Scates

Winning Volleyball

WINNING VOLLEYBALL

Fundamentals, Tactics and Strategy

ALLEN E. SCATES

University of California
USA 1971 Pan American Team Coach
USA 1972 Olympic Team Coach

ALLYN AND BACON   BOSTON

To my loving wife SUE.

Thank you for your patience.

Library of Congress Catalog Number: 70-162880

Contents

Acknowledgments   **vi**
Preface   **vii**

I INTRODUCTION

1 Development and History   **3**

    Origin and Development
    The History of Volleyball Rules
    The Modern Game
    National Organizations
    International Competition

II FUNDAMENTALS

2 The Serve   **21**

    Underhand Serve
    Overhand Serve
    Round House Serve
    Serving Drills

3 The Pass   **31**

    The Pass
    Hand Position

Arm Position
Passing Techniques
Moving to the Ball
Changing Direction
Lateral Pass
One-Arm Pass
Backward Pass
Unexpected Positions

4 The Set   49

Front Set
Back Set
Lateral Set
Traditional Setting Position
Strategy
Teaching Progression
For Setting Specialists

5 The Spike   69

The Dink
Off-Speed Spike
Spiking the Low Vertical Set
Spiking a Shoot Set
Spiking Drills

6 The Block   105

Individual Blocking Technique
Attack Block
Soft Block
Two-Man Block
Blocking Strategy
Reading the Spiker
Common Errors
Teaching Progression
Game Situation Drills

7 Individual Defensive Technique   135

Stance
One-Arm Dig
Overhand Dig
Diving
Body Position
Moving to the Ball
Learning the Dive

III TEAM PLAY

8 Offense   163

Two-Hitter Attack
M-Formation
Three-Hitter Attack
Five-One Attack

9 Defense   183

Starting Positions
Middle Back Defense
Defensing the Center Spiker
Middle Back Defense to Offense
Middle In Defense
Stopping the Center Attack
Middle In Defense to Offense
Changing Defenses

10 Coeducational and Doubles Play   203

Coeducational Play
Doubles Play
Beach Doubles

IV ORGANIZATION

11 Training and Conditioning   215

Conditioning Programs
Seasonal Training Cycle
Weekly and Daily Schedule

12 Responsibilities of the Coach

Philosophy
Practice Sessions
We Will Do What Is Impossible
Scouting and Statistics
Home Team Receiving Chart
Opponent Passing Chart
Attack Chart
The Game

Appendix   251

Index

Acknowledgments

To the contributing photographers

DR. LEONARD STALLCUP, Official USVBA Photographer

STAN TROUTMAN, UCLA

BUD FIELDS

BOB VAN WAGNER

GARY ADAMS, *Beverly Hills Independent*

LURLINE K. FUJII

Many photographs are reproduced by courtesy of the Ealing Corporation and the Los Angeles City Unified School District.

To the players on the UCLA Bruins, the men and women of the United States Volleyball Association and the children in the Beverly Hills School District for their excellent demonstration of the fundamentals of the game.

To Coaches

HARRY E. WILSON

GLEN EGSTROM

BURT DE GROOT

VAL KELLER

TOSHI TOYODA

J. D. MORGAN, UCLA Athletic Director

To ESTHER GOLDFARB, who typed and edited much of the manuscript.

Preface

Volleyball is played in over 100 countries using standard international rules. The Athletic Institute reports 60 million volleyball participants in the United States alone. Volleyball is a physically demanding game with plays and patterns that rival basketball for intricacy and imagination. Within the last few years the NCAA, NAIA and DGWS have all adopted volleyball as a championship event.

Winning Volleyball is the complete guide for the player, teacher and coach who want a comprehensive insight into the many changes in fundamentals, tactics and strategy that have occurred since volleyball has become an Olympic sport. To date it is the most readable, well-illustrated book written on American volleyball. All ideas reflected in the book are designed for both male and female players unless specifically noted.

Six of the twelve chapters are devoted to helping the beginner master the latest fundamental techniques that are used at all levels of competition. Step-by-step learning sequences and drills are included to improve performance. Hundreds of easy-to-follow sequence and action photographs of All American and Olympic men and women clearly illustrate techniques. The coverage of the serve, pass, set, spike, block and individual defensive techniques give the prospective player or established coach the insight into the basic principles required for successful play. These fundamental techniques should not be considered too advanced for the average player.

There are detailed sections on duration and intensity of practice sessions, selection of offense and defense, and scouting and game plans. All standard offenses and defenses and serve reception patterns are covered. This material is more advanced than anything else presently being offered by American authors. It is a necessity for serious students in the game. After studying this book the reader should be qualified to become a teacher or coach at any level of play.

Part I

INTRODUCTION

1

Development and History

The status of volleyball has increased tremendously since it was adopted as an Olympic sport in 1964. The sensational play of the 1964 Gold Medalist Japanese Women's team opened the door to mass exposure of the sport via television, film and subsequent tours of foreign teams throughout the Southern Hemisphere.

The Japanese men and women use the greatest individual and team defenses known to the game. The women have perfected the *rolling dig*, which enables them to go to the floor and retrieve a hard hit spike and then roll to their feet in time for the next play. The Japanese men have perfected the spectacular *diving save*, which provides even greater court coverage and makes their defense almost impenetrable.

Volleyball was slow to develop in this country because of its image as a nonstrenuous game in which a ball was lobbed back and forth across a low net. Today the game of "power" volleyball demands a player who can dive or roll to the floor to recover his opponent's attack and jump high above the net to block or spike a moving ball into his opponent's court. Power volleyball

> differs from recreational volleyball in the amount of organization necessary for the highly refined application of team strategy and individual skills. Power volleyball demands a quick and alert, extremely well-coordinated athlete, with great stamina to master its complex skills and playing situations.[1]

During the past few years, new standards of volleyball training and performance have emerged to test the speed, strength, endurance and coordination of the best athletes. The sport has begun to assume a position of importance in the eyes of students and athletic departments throughout the country.

In 1969 the National Association of Intercollegiate Athletics (NAIA) adopted volleyball as an official NAIA championship event and held its first tournament at George Williams College in Chicago. In 1970 the National Collegiate Athletic Association (NCAA) and Division of Girls and Women's Sports held national championships. During that same year, for the first time in its history, the Amateur Athletic Union (AAU) national championships included an Academic Boys and Academic Girls division for secondary school youngsters.

During the 1968/69 school year there were 3,312 high schools being represented by 59,132 players in interscholastic competition.[2]

The universal game of volleyball can be adapted to the needs and ability of any participant. Lowering of the net at the elementary level, lenient interpretation of the rules for recreational play and modified rules for coeducational volleyball appeal to people of all ages at different levels of skill.

ORIGIN AND DEVELOPMENT

In 1895, William G. Morgan, a YMCA physical director in Holyoke, Massachusetts, devised the game of volleyball (first called *mintonette*).[3] He strung a lawn tennis net at a height of 6 ft. 6 in. across the gym and used the inside of a basketball for the ball. The game was invented to provide an activity for middle aged businessmen that was competitive, fun and not too strenuous. In 1896, Morgan put on a demonstration for a conference of YMCA physical directors at Springfield, and Professor Alfred T. Halstead of Springfield College renamed the game *volleyball*.[4] Mr. Morgan's volleyball rules were published in 1897 in the *Handbook of the Athletic League of YMCA's of North America*.[5] During the next several years, YMCA physical directors introduced the game throughout the United States and in many foreign countries. In 1913, volleyball was included in the Far Eastern Games in Manila by Elwood S. Brown, the International YMCA Secretary. In 1916 the *Spaulding Volleyball Rule Book* was published at the request of the YMCA, and the NCAA was invited to help promote the game. In an article in the *1916 Volleyball Official Guide*, it was estimated that 200,000 persons in the United States played volleyball.[6] During World War I, "more than 16,000 volleyballs were distributed in 1919 to the American Expeditionary Forces alone."[7]

The United States Volleyball Association (USVBA) was formed in 1928, and the previously closed National YMCA Championship became open to teams from other organizations. To this day, USVBA Open Championships are held in conjunction with YMCA championships. The first senior championship for men 35 years or older also began during this year.

United States Armed Forces stretched a rope or net between supports and played volleyball during rest periods in World War II. The sight of American soldiers playing volleyball helped the sport's growth and world-wide popularity.

It was estimated that within two years after the close of the war the number of volleyball players doubled and some five to ten million participants were active in the United States alone.[8]

The International Volleyball Federation (FIVB) was formed in 1947 and the USVBA was a charter member. In 1948 the USA volleyball team made a good-will tour of Europe. The USVBA sponsored separate college and women's divisions in the 1949 championships held in Los Angeles. The University of Southern California won the Collegiate Division and Houston, Texas won the Women's Division.[9] Los Alamitos Naval Air Station won the first Inter-service Volleyball Championship held in Columbus, Ohio during 1952.[10] Volleyball was included in the 1955 Pan American Games in Mexico City. Mexico won and the USA placed second. In 1964, volleyball took a monumental step forward when it was included in the Olympic Games held in Tokyo, Japan. It was included in the Olympics because it had become one of the most popular sports in the world—"more than eighty countries play volleyball, with some 25 recognizing the game as a major sport."[11]

The game is very popular in Eastern Europe and in the Far East. The USSR and Czechoslovakia have dominated the men's international competition, while the USSR and Japan have dominated the women's international competition thus far.

THE HISTORY OF VOLLEYBALL RULES

In a recent article in the *Official USVBA Volleyball Guide*, Dr. William T. Odeneal* outlined the basic features of the original rules written by William Morgan in 1895.[12]

- Net, 6 ft. 6 in.
- Court, 25 ft. by 50 ft.
- Any number of participants allowed
- Length of game, nine innings; each team allowed three outs per inning
- Continuous air dribbling of ball permitted up to a restraining line 4 ft. from the net
- Unlimited number of hits allowed on each side of court
- A served ball can be assisted across the net
- Second serve allowed (as in tennis) if first serve results in a fault

---

*William T. Odeneal's doctoral dissertation is titled *The History and Contributions of the United States Volleyball Association*. He was formerly the coach of the USVBA Collegiate Champion Florida State University Volleyball Team and is presently a member of the NCAA Volleyball Tournament Committee.

● Any ball hitting net (except on first serve) is a fault, resulting in a side out

Obviously, drastic changes have occurred since Mr. Morgan demonstrated the game to his YMCA associates at Springfield College.

The following lists outline the changes which have taken place and govern the game as it is played in the United States today. Some of these changes were deleted for a number of years, but were reinstated at a later date.

1912

● 6 players on each side

1915

● Official timer

1916

● Official game, 15 points
● Two out of three games determine a match
● Height of net, 8 ft.
● Player rotation; each player serves in turn
● Any serve that touches the net or any outside object considered out of bounds
● Ball not allowed to rest in a player's hands
● No playing the ball a second time unless played by another player

The rules were published in a separate book, *Official Volleyball Rules.*

1920

● Ball may be touched by any part of body above the waist
● Court size, 30 ft. by 60 ft.
● Before crossing net, ball may be played three times by each team

1922

● Center line under net
● Scorer
● Double foul defined and written in rules

1923

● 6 players per team, 12 players per squad
● Players are numbered
● Player in right back position serves

1925

- Umpire
- Player must obtain referee's permission to leave court
- Ball must cross net over side line
- Each team allowed two time outs per game
- Team having a 2-point advantage wins a 14-14 tie game

1926

- Court measured to outside edges of boundary lines
- Length of net, 32 ft.
- Game *forfeited* if either team is reduced to less than 6 players

1932

- Center line extended indefinitely; player allowed outside of court to make play
- Vertical tape marker put on net over side lines

1935

- Players required to wear numbers on shirts
- Touching the net—a foul

1937

- Not a foul if ball driven into net causes net to come in contact with player
- Multiple contacts allowed in receiving a hard-driven spike

1942

- Forfeited game score, 15–0

1948

- Service area, right third of court
- Simultaneous contacts by two players constitute one hit

1950

- Clarification of a *held ball* stipulates that ball must be clearly batted

1952

- Players allowed to warm up during time outs

1953

- Substitutes allowed to re-enter game twice

1954

- Players must remain in position until ball is struck for serve

1956

- Players may stand anywhere on court, provided they are in rotation order
- Teams allowed to change courts during third game of a match if 4 minutes of ball in play have expired, or if one team has scored 8 points

1960

- Net height for women, 7 ft. 4 1/4 in.

1962

- Players not allowed to grab officials' platform to halt themselves from going over center line

1965

- Players may cross assumed extension line, provided they do not attempt to play the ball
- Illegal to screen receivers from server

1968

- Minimum ceiling height, 26 ft.
- Lines added to outline 10-ft. serving area on right side of court
- Spiking line moved from 7 1/2 ft. to 10 ft. back from net; back line spikers allowed to land in front of spiking line, provided they leave the floor behind it
- Ball cannot be played with any part of body below waist
- Blockers may reach across net, provided they do not contact ball until it has been attacked
- An individual blocker may contact ball twice in succession
- Players may follow through over the net when returning the ball

1969

- Teams limited to 12 substitutions per game

- Blocking permitted by front line players only
- If two opponents simultaneously hit ball above net, the player behind the direction of the ball is considered to have touched it last
- If two opponents hold ball simultaneously, it is a double fault and a play-over

1970

- Width of center line increased from 2 in. to 4 in.
- Umpire's duties increased at discretion of referee
- Injured player must be replaced by a substitute immediately
- No change in line-up allowed when team has been signaled to take the court
- Ball may or may not be tossed in air before striking it for a serve

1971

- Blocking rules clarified and interpretations refined
- Serve cannot be blocked *across* net
- Any ball but the serve may be played off the ceiling, fixtures or other obstructions if these intrude on court's height; however, no such ball may rebound into opponents' court
- Ball declared *dead* if it comes to rest or is wedged in ceiling or other obstruction
- Height of net for elementary school children—no lower than 6 ft.
- *Coed play*—one backcourt player may also block when there is only one male player in a front line position

THE MODERN GAME

The game of power volleyball in the United States has changed significantly during the past five years. A majority of the better teams are using a three-hitter offense, which features a variety of sets and spikes designed around fast patterns of attack. There is increased emphasis on the defensive techniques of diving and rolling to the floor to dig or retrieve balls; these tactics, in turn, have led to longer rallies. Recent rule changes and interpretations have allowed officials to silence their whistles and let the players determine the outcome of the game.

In the United States, volleyball is the most popular of the participant sports and is fast becoming a popular spectator sport as well.

Effects of Recent Rule Changes

The time-consuming ritual of having five players form a screen in front of the server to hide the ball from the receiving team was outlawed in 1965. At one time, screening players were actually allowed to wave their arms in a distracting manner to confuse their opponents. Often, the receiver could not see a small server at all—nor could he see the flight of the serve until it came into view just before crossing the net. Naturally, the accuracy of the pass was impaired, which proved to be a great handicap to the few teams that needed a precise pass to utilize their three-hitter offense.

It was not unusual for a server to change his position from the right to the middle or left of the serving area. Until 1968, this serving area extended across the entire back line. The server often moved the screen about in a comical parade until the chosen receiver was isolated behind a wall of players.

Today's rules call for the server to put the ball into play without undue delay when the referee blows his whistle and calls for the serve. The server must be in the serving area behind the end line in the right third of the court. Players are not allowed to screen or raise their arms to confuse the receiver. Teams now practice receiving the serve from one area of the court and consequently pass the serve with greater accuracy. This allows the setters to arrive under the ball in position and watch the approaching spiker and the blockers. Thus, the skilled setter can deliver a variety of "play sets" to deceive the opponents' block.

The rule that significantly changed the game allows the blockers to reach across the net to contact the ball after the offense has attacked it. This forces opposing setters to pull the sets back from the net and prevent the blockers from forming a "roof" around the set and stuffing the spike to the floor. Since the spikers must contact the ball further away from the net, the spike has to travel in a flatter trajectory instead of being hit straight down in their opponents' court. Spikers can no longer jump up and hit the ball as hard as possible in attempting to overpower the block.

Successful spikers learn to place the ball past the blockers using a variety of spiking angles and a change of pace dink shot and/or off-speed spike. The fast and well-coordinated "digger" has more time to react to spikes which are of necessity hit flatter and deeper into the court. Every good player must learn to dive to recover dink shots and half-speed spikes which fall in front of him.

Individual blockers are allowed to contact the ball twice in succession instead of standing helpless as their blocked ball drops to the floor. Long rallies are common with the liberalized blocking rules, and the dive and roll have become a common defensive fundamental. Players are no longer cheered when they hit the floor to retreive a ball; they are expected to do so. The ball is dead when contacted below the waist, and the few remaining players who preferred to kick at a low ball rather than go on the floor have been forced to learn the new techniques. Emphasis on over-all conditioning and increasing the vertical jump through weight training have become popular with serious volleyball athletes.

The four-man block that hindered the three-hitter attack was abolished in 1969, and only front row players are now allowed to block. Teams that can pass the ball accurately will usually enjoy one-on-one blocking situations against their three-hitter attack.

When a backcourt player was allowed to join three front court teammates at the net to block, it was difficult, regardless of the play, for a spiker in a three-hitter attack to isolate himself in a one-on-one situation. Four blockers spaced evenly across the court always enjoyed a tactical advantage at the net. It was feared this rule change would legislate against the small player who, under the previous rulings, could switch to the backcourt to dig and allow a taller player to take his place at the net.

This rule, however, has forced players to become skilled in all defensive aspects of the game. The tall and clumsy player who switched to an end blocking position in all three backcourt positions had to learn to play backcourt defense. The small setter who switched to the backcourt had to learn to block effectively. Smaller players have not vanished from the sport; they have increased their vertical jump by better techniques or weight training, or a combination of both. The tall and slow spiker has either improved defensive skills or has been relegated to the in position on the middle in defense where fewer digging skills are needed.

The spiker is allowed to reach over the net when following through after contacting the ball. This relieves the referee of stopping the play every time an offensive player's hand incidentally flicks across the net.

Effects of Recent Rule Interpretations

The overhand pass of the serve in power volleyball is a rarity. At recent USVBA and NCAA championships, approximately 99 percent of the serves were passed with the forearms. Coaches do not teach the overhand pass, and players only practice this technique for purposes of setting. International referees called overhand reception of the serve very tightly before and during the 1964 Olympics. When Olympic players representing the United States returned home, they used the forearm pass exclusively to prevent the officials from calling a thrown ball. Leading coaches reasoned that officials would closely scrutinize the overhand pass while rarely calling a rule infraction on the "bump" or forearm pass. It is good percentage play to teach the forearm pass and to move the receiving players deeper in the court so that they can bump every serve.

Recent directives from the USVBA and the International Volleyball Federation have reminded referees and players that overhand service reception is legal; but, the current players have perfected the forearm pass until it is possible to bump the ball with such accuracy that there is virtually no advantage in returning to the old method. One benefit from the spectators' standpoint is that the referee's whistle has been noticeably quiet during service reception.

Upon returning home from the 1964 Olympics, United States players, coaches and referees were astonished at the officials' leniency during the set. The foreign officials seemed to automatically call every overhand service reception a thrown ball, and then shut their eyes at the manner in which the setters were delivering the ball. *The international setters had learned to set the ball from any body position in any direction!* Blockers from the United

States were confused by the setters' maneuvers and seemed to be continually late in reaching their blocking assignments.

American setters had been taught to stand with their shoulders at a right angle to the net and set the ball directly forward or backward. Since the USVBA rules had not yet incorporated the interpretations of the International Volleyball Federation, American setters had been taught to release the ball with a flick of the wrist. This meant that they contacted the ball and released it immediately. Although the American players had a beautiful "touch" on the ball, they had not learned to keep the ball in contact with their fingers as long as the foreign setters.

The obvious advantages of a prolonged contact of the ball are increased options of direction and greater accuracy of the set. The foreign setters could accomplish prolonged contact by keeping their elbows closer to the sides of their body and by relying on greater arm and hand action to deliver the set. After exposure to the advantageous international style of setting, the better setters from the United States worked to master international techniques; and, United States National Officials became more liberal in their interpretations of what constituted a thrown ball.

Although USVBA rules still state that the ball must be clearly hit and cannot visibly come to rest at contact, current interpretation falls between the leniency shown in international play and pre-1964 competition in the USA.

> For example, the ball does not have to travel in the direction the body is facing as long as there is an immediate contact and release with little or no follow-through by the hands and arms.[13]

In the 1963 Pan American Games, 1964 Olympics and subsequent International Competition, players representing the United States became exposed to half-speed spikes and open-hand dink or placement shots. Since the international spikers had been confronted by opponents reaching over the net to block, they had developed alternate methods of attack to complement the hard spike. These off-speed shots caught the American backcourt players flat-footed, as they were interpreted as thrown balls in national competition within the United States. Returning Olympians developed these techniques of attack and used them frequently enough to force opposing players to learn to dive and roll to the floor to retrieve these shots.

National Officials, who would have whistled lesser-known spikers off the court for having used open-hand dinks and half-speed spikes with prolonged hand contact, gradually liberalized their interpretation of what constituted a thrown ball during the attack. These methods soon became accepted practice. Before these techniques of attack became popular, a player would go to the floor to retrieve a ball only if he were out of position or had tripped. Today, the spiker may dink the ball with his fingertips and

> change the course of the ball by directing it across the body, if the change of direction does not come from a break or follow-through of the wrist.[14]

NATIONAL ORGANIZATIONS

United States Volleyball Association (USVBA)

The USVBA is recognized by the United States Olympic Committee as the governing body for volleyball in this country. It is strictly a volunteer organization that consists of an executive committee, 15 standing committee chairmen and over 100 standing committee members.[15] The YMCA has supplied integral leadership in this organization, which was formed in 1928. Many of these volunteers are retired players who wish to stay close to the game and do so by accepting committee or officiating assignments.

The USVBA registers its own players and regulates all eligibility procedures for organizations, teams and individuals competing in its local, regional and national tournaments. Each year the organization arrives at a different site and conducts a double elimination national championship for Open Men, Open Women, Men's Collegiate*and Senior Men's divisions. The National YMCA Championship is awarded to the YMCA team that finishes highest in the National Open Championships. The USVBA Championships are held Wednesday through Saturday during the first week in May and generally accept a total of about 80 entries.

National Collegiate Athletic Association (NCAA)

The NCAA conducts 27 national championships in 18 sports for its more than 700 colleges, universities and affiliated associations. Nine tournaments are held separately at the university and college level, and volleyball is one of the 18 combined championship events. "Nearly 5000 athletes compete annually in NCAA-sponsored events."[17]

In 1969, 41 colleges had participated in USVBA-sanctioned tournaments[18]; at that time, only 28 NCAA colleges were sponsored by their athletic departments. After the announcement by the NCAA that volleyball would be conducted as one of the annual championship events, 45 additional member institutions indicated that their teams might receive athletic department sponsorship in the future, with 33 projecting teams by 1973-1974.[19]

---

*In 1970 the Men's Collegiate was discontinued because the National Collegiate Athletic Association (NCAA) and National Association of Intercollegiate Athletics (NAIA) colleges were sending teams to their own championship events. The USVBA Collegiate Committee reinstated the Men's Collegiate Division in 1971 primarily for two-year colleges and unaffiliated four-year colleges.

The USVBA holds clinics throughout the country and sends teams abroad to play in major international volleyball events. Due largely to the efforts of the USVBA, volleyball has become the greatest participant sport in the USA, with 60,000,000 participants.[16]

The USVBA publishes an *Annual Official Volleyball Rules and Reference Guide.* These rules are adopted by the NCAA, NAIA, Amateur Athletic Union (AAU) and almost every other organization that sponsors volleyball competition in the USA. With a few exceptions, such as substituting, these are the same International Rules followed by every country in the world.

In 1970, Pepperdine College in Los Angeles became the first institution in the United States to hire a head coach from the Far East. Moo Park became the director of this school's new intercollegiate volleyball program.

In 1968, Moo Park coached his team to the Korean National Championship, and immediately, was named coach of the '68 Korean Olympic Team.[20]

Division for Girls and Women's Sports (DGWS)

The [DGWS] is a nonprofit educational organization designed to serve the needs and interests of administrators, teachers, leaders and participants in sports programs for girls and women. Active members of the Division are women members of the American Association for Health, Physical Education, and Recreation who are interested in sports for girls and women who participate in the work of the Division.[21]

The first intercollegiate volleyball national championships for women were held at California State College Long Beach, April 23-25, 1970, and were sponsored by the DGWS. Twenty-eight top-ranking teams from such states as California, New Mexico, Oregon, Florida, Ohio, Mississippi, Missouri, Illinois, Utah and Texas were represented.[22] Several former Olympians and USVBA All Americans competed for their college teams. Sul Ross State University in Alpine, Texas, emerged as the first DGWS champion.

National Association of Intercollegiate Athletics (NAIA)

The first national intercollegiate volleyball tournament sponsored by a national collegiate governing body was hosted by George Williams College in Downers Grove, Illinois, May 2-3, 1969. The seven-team double elimination NAIA volleyball championship "was won by Earlham College, Richmond, Indiana, with Indiana Tech, Ft. Wayne, Indiana, finishing second."[23]

The NAIA was officially organized in 1940 and sponsors 17 annual national championships for its 550 colleges and universities.

The prime objective of the NAIA is to champion the cause and promote the interests of the college of moderate enrollment and sound athletic policy and program.[24]

Amateur Athletic Union (AAU)

The AAU has held 28 national championships since 1925. The AAU usually holds its tournament a few days before the USVBA Championships and chooses a location near the USVBA site. This tournament attracts a number of teams which desire a final tune-up before the USVBA Championships. Teams in this tournament are usually at partial strength, as many players are not willing to take the additional expense and time away from their jobs or schools to compete in both championships.

High School

The National Federation of State High School Athletic Associations conducted a Sports Participation Survey for 1968-1969, which indicated that "there were 3,312 high schools being represented by 59,132 youngsters in interscholastic volleyball."[25] Texas led the nation with 986 schools (19,998 participants) sponsoring interscholastic volleyball.

Other Groups

The Mormons have held an annual national volleyball championship since 1950. During the 1968 Olympic year, over 2,500 junior and senior men's teams competed in thirty-seven zones throughout the United States and Canada. Junior and senior zone champions competed in a two-day double elimination tournament in Salt Lake City.[26]

Other groups that hold volleyball championships are the American Turners, Jewish Welfare Board, American Latvian Association, Army, Navy, Air Force and Marines. The Catholic Youth Organization (CYO) is very active in local competition.

INTERNATIONAL COMPETITION

United States Olympic Committee

The Men and Women's Olympic Volleyball Committee selects players, coaches, managers and officials to participate in the Pan American and Olympic Games. Sixteen members out of 30 on the Men's Committee are representatives from the USVBA; 20 out of 29 are representatives from the USVBA on the Women's Committee. Other organizations such as the NCAA, NAIA, Armed Forces and AAHPER (DGWS) have representatives on the committees.

International Volleyball Federation (FIVB)

Olympic Games, Pan American Games, World Games, international matches and all play outside of the United States use the playing rules of the International Volleyball Federation. Within the last few years the USVBA has made several rule changes to bring the two sets of rules closer together. In both USVBA and International Rules, the only exception for women is a lowering of the net.

The Federation International Volley Ball (FIVB) holds volleyball competition that is stronger than that in the Olympic Games. Since a maximum of eight to twelve men's teams and six to eight women's teams have been allowed in the Olympics, many of the world's better teams are eliminated in tough zone competition and fail to earn a berth in the Olympics. For example, men's world volleyball powers such as Romania and Yugoslavia had been considered among the top ten in International Competition but were rated behind Russia, Czechoslovakia, East Germany and Poland; and they did not receive an invitation to represent their zone in the 1968 Olympics in Mexico City. These teams always compete in the World Games, however.

The United States has not participated in several FIVB Championships because necessary funds were not raised to send teams.

United States Collegiate Sports Council (USCSC)

In 1967 the USCSC was founded by the following organizations:

- National Junior College Athletic Association
- United States National Student Association
- National Association of Intercollegiate Athletics (NAIA)
- The National Collegiate Athletic Association (NCAA)
- American Association for Health, Physical Education, and Recreation

The primary purpose of the Council is to promote international collegiate sport through increased participation of American student athletes in the World University Games. The World University Games is a major biennial competition sponsored by the IUSF, with membership of over 50 countries. The Volleyball Games Committee of the USCSC was formed to select men and women student-athletes and coaches from colleges in the United States to compete in this world competition.

REFERENCES

1. United States Volleyball Association. 1968. *It's power volleyball.* Edited by Carl M. McGowan. See p. 4. Distributed through the office of Mrs. Betty Ghormley, P. O. Box 514, Pacific Palisades, Calif. 90272.

2. Arnold, David C. 1969. *High school interscholastic status.* A report to the USVBA committee on Organizational Relationships by the Assistant Executive Secretary National Federation-State High School Athletic Associations.

3. Friermood, Harold T. Volleyball reflections. In *1970 official volleyball guide.* Berne, Ind.: United States Volleyball Association. See pp. 144-149.

4. Ibid.

5. Friermood, Harold T. (Ed.) 1966. *When volleyball began--An Olympic sport.* Berne, Ind.: United States Volleyball Association. 90 pages. A complete reproduction of the *1916 Spaulding Volleyball Guide* and selected highlights.

6. Friermood, Volleyball reflections.

7. Friermood, *When volleyball began.*

8. McGowan. *It's power volleyball.*

9. Friermood, Harold T. Cumulative record of volleyball championship

winners. In *1969 official volleyball guide*. Berne, Ind.: United States Volleyball Association. See pp. 105-121.

10. Friermood, Volleyball reflections.

11. McGowan. *It's power volleyball*. See p. 2.

12. Odeneal, William T. A summary of seventy five years of rules. In *1970 official volleyball guide*. Berne, Ind.: United States Volleyball Association. See pp. 149-154.

13. Scates, Allen E., and Ward, Jane. 1969. *Volleyball*. Boston: Allyn and Bacon. See pp. 37 and 38.

14. Ibid.

15. Boyden, Doug. A departing challenge. In *1970 official volleyball guide*. Berne, Ind.: United States Volleyball Association. See pp. 6-8.

16. Wilson, Harry E. President's message. In *1970 official volleyball guide*. Berne, Ind.: United States Volleyball Association. See p. 10.

17. *1970-71 NCAA manual*. The National Collegiate Athletic Association, 1221 Baltimore Ave., Kansas City, Mo. 64105.

18. Baird, W. W. *Post-nationals bulletin to regional commissioners and friends*. A report from the National Commissioner of Regions, United States Volleyball Association.

19. Foley, Jon A. (NCAA Promotion Director). 20 February 1970, personal correspondence with the author.

20. Mazza, Bob. Pepperdine hires Korean Olympic volleyball coach. 1 July 1970, publicity release.

21. Stauff, Marilyn (Ed.) *1969-1971 volleyball guide*. The Division for Girls' and Women's Sports, 1201 Sixteenth St., N. W., Washington, D. C.

22. Dossey, Lyndee (Publicity Chairman DGWS National Intercollegiate Volleyball Championships). 30 March 1970, personal correspondence with the author.

23. McNamara, Jerre. Earlham College wins National Association of Intercollegiate Athletics National Volleyball Championships. In *1970 official volleyball guide*. Berne, Ind.: United States Volleyball Association. See p. 128.

24. *The 1969-1970 national directory of college athletics*. 1969. Roy Franks Publishing Ranch, Box 7068, Amarillo, Texas 79108. See p. 36.

25. Arnold. *High school*.

26. Mills, Wayne. All Church Mormon Volleyball Championships. In *1969 official volleyball guide*. (Berne, Ind.: United States Volleyball Association). See p. 146.

Part II

FUNDAMENTALS

2

The Serve

With his hand, fist or arm, the *server* hits the ball over the net into the opponents' area of the court. The right back player on the serving team is the first
server of the game. This player continues to serve until his team commits a
foul or the game is completed. If a member of the serving team commits a
foul, a side out is called by the referee and the ball is awarded to the opponents, who rotate clockwise one position. The player rotating from the right
front position is always the next server.

a   b

Fig. 2.1 The Serve   *Servers sometimes stand 20–30 ft. behind the end
line so that they can hit the ball with great force and still keep the serve in
their opponents' court. Both girls toss the ball above and in front of their
serving shoulder, transferring their weight from their back to front leg before contacting the ball. (Dr. Leonard Stallcup)*

The service area is located in the right third of the court behind the end line. The server cannot touch the lines bounding this area or the floor outside the service area until after the ball is contacted. However, the server's arm or body may be in the air over or beyond these lines. In the event the playing area does not extend to a minimum depth of 6 ft. beyond the end line, the server is allowed to step into the court to whatever distance is necessary for providing the minimum service area.

Players should develop a serve that can put their opponents on the defensive by accurate placement, unpredictable movement, high velocity or a combination of these factors. Players on the varsity level should be able to deliver their strongest serves to their opponents' court in at least nine out of ten attempts.

UNDERHAND SERVE

The underhand serve is the easiest to learn and control. It requires very little strength in comparison to the other serves and can be mastered by most elementary school children. The exceptionally weak or uncoordinated child should be allowed to serve in front of the serving line during games, and gradually move back to the regulation 30-ft. serving line as his skill and confidence improve.

a   *b*

Fig. 2.2 Underhand Serve   *Striking the ball on its right side will cause it to travel to the player's left or cross court (a). Notice that this player's serving arm follows through slightly across his body (b). When striking the ball on its right or left side is mastered, the position of the body can remain the same regardless of where the server intends to direct the ball. This same principle applies to the round house serves. (Ealing Corp.)*

Unlike the overhand serve, the underhand serve is not a strong weapon. When accurately placed and carrying a "floating" motion, however, it can threaten the opposition.

The server places his left foot forward and bends both knees slightly. He takes a long backswing with his striking arm and contacts the ball below the midline with the heel of his hand (if the hand is open) or with the heel and knuckles (if the hand is closed). If the server prematurely takes his eyes off the ball, he may contact the ball above its midline and serve into the net. The server's weight shifts from the back leg to the forward one at the moment of contact. Follow-through occurs in the direction of flight.

When follow-through is not in a straight line, it indicates that the arm-swing was outside in or inside out; thus, the ball travels past the side lines and is out of bounds. When the ball is contacted too far below the midline, it is caused by a flexing of the ball-holding arm just prior to contact. Beginners tend to raise their ball-holding arm when extending their knees before hitting the ball.

OVERHAND SERVE

Overhand floater serve

The overhand "floater" serve, having no spin, moves in an erratic path as it approaches the receiver. It is difficult to pass. To achieve the desired floating action, the ball is hit with only a momentary point of contact with very little follow-through. This quick contact just below the center of the ball causes it to travel with a "wiggle" type of motion—rising, dropping or moving from side to side—similar to a knuckleball in baseball. At recent USVBA, NCAA, NAIA and DGWS championships, about 95 percent of the serves were overhand floater serves.

If the floater serve does not have any "action," or wiggle-type movement on the ball, the server has usually contacted the ball with too large an area of his hand, snapped his wrist or used too much follow-through. The majority of servers hit the ball with the heel of the hand. Some, however, strike the ball with the heel of the hand and closed fingers, or a closed fist. Tall players generally prefer to bend their arm slightly on contact. For additional power, many servers take a short step forward with their front foot just prior to contact.

In Fig. 2.3, Olympian Patti Bright holds the ball about shoulder height, directly in line with her back foot. Her feet are in a stride position and her weight is evenly distributed. She tosses the ball about 3 ft. in the air, above and in front of her right shoulder. Her right arm extends from a cocked position to contact the ball a few inches below its midline with the heel of her hand. Patti is short; therefore, she fully extends her right arm upon contact with the ball so that it will travel in a low trajectory and still clear the net. Notice that her wrist is stiff and that there is little follow-through.

The area of the ball housing the valve stem is heavier than the rest of the

a b c

d e

Fig. 2.3 Overhand Floater Serve *Olympian Patti Bright demonstrates the overhand floater serve. (Los Angeles City Unified School District)*

ball, which causes an uneven distribution of weight. Since the official volleyball only weighs about 9 ounces, this valve stem usually causes the ball to break in its direction during the floater serve. Many coaches believe that the air hits the valve as the ball travels along its flight, causing the ball to wobble and move about.

Regardless of which theory or combination of factors are at work, the placement of the valve upon contact does have an effect on the flight of the ball. Experience has shown that if the valve is pointed toward the center of the serving target, the ball will break from side to side. When the valve is pointed down, the ball will drop and when the valve is pointed up, the ball will travel a greater distance.

When using the common serving strategy of serving the "seams" of two receivers' area of responsibility, many servers place the valve on the weaker receiver's side so that the serve will break in that direction. Of course, the toss must be perfected to place the valve stem in the proper position.

Many players disregard the location of the valve stem and consequently lose some accuracy during the serve. Players should experiment with the valve placement during practice sessions to make their serves harder to receive.

Fig. 2.4 Valve Placement
Placing the valve toward the opponents' floor will help the floater serve move from side to side with a dropping action. (Ealing Corp.)

Overhand spin serve

The overhand spin serve results in a fast dropping action, which gives the opposition less time to react. Although quite effective when used against inexperienced competition, better players find the flight of the ball very predictable (due to its spinning action) and usually have little trouble in passing the serve. It is difficult for most servers to control the spin serve, and it is not popular because of the increased chance of a serving error.

During the past decade, Gene Selznick, Randy Carter, Mary Jo Peppler and Larry Rundle were the only outstanding players in this country to develop the accuracy and speed needed to score frequently with this serve in important competition.

The right-handed server places his left foot in front and stands in a stride position. He tosses the ball about 4 ft. in the air (one foot higher than the toss for the floater). The server's left arm should be fully extended as his right arm, hand held open, cocks behind his head. Shoulders rotate so that his left shoulder faces the net and weight is on the back foot. As the ball starts to descend, his shoulders twist forward and the elbow leads the way as his arm begins to straighten. The ball is contacted on the lower midsection in the center; the heel of the server's hand first contacts the ball, and then the wrist snap rolls his hand over the ball, imparting topspin as weight shifts to the forward foot.

The server may contact the ball on the left or right side, causing the ball to curve. Since the server must stand behind the right third of the court, right-handed players usually strike the ball on the right side so the ball will not fly beyond the near side line.

ROUND HOUSE SERVE

The underhand serve is still used by the majority of players participating in recreational volleyball in this country. Athletes participating in "power" volleyball, where a refined application of team strategy and individual skills are required, overwhelmingly prefer the overhand floater serve. Europeans participating in power volleyball have used the round house and overhand spin and, to a lesser extent, the overhand floater serve.

Fig. 2.5 Overhand Spin Serve *This serve results in a fast dropping action that gives the passer less time to react. All World Gene Selznick prepares to contact the ball slightly on the right side to impart a curving action. (Dr. Leonard Stallcup)*

Until a few years ago the serve was the only fundamental area of the game in which the American teams consistently outperformed the Europeans in international competition. Recently, the improved technique utilized in the forearm pass by the Europeans has negated the slight serving advantage that the Americans once enjoyed. United States national teams have not experienced any great difficulty when receiving the fast and predictable round house and overhand spin serves of the Europeans. Consequently, our top players have not used these serves.

a   b

Fig. 2.6 Toss   *As he tosses the ball, the player leans over his back leg. His serving arm extends downward. His arm moves in a windmill action, and the ball is contacted directly over the hitting shoulder. (Ealing Corp.)*

In 1960 the Japanese Women's team introduced the round house floater serve in international competition at the World Volleyball Championships in Brazil. Since their opponents did not have an opportunity to practice against the hard, fast-floating action of this serve, it was an instant success. After the Japanese Women's team won the Gold Medal in the 1964 Olympic Games in Tokyo, they made numerous tours in the United States to compete against our top women players. After attempting to field the superior serves of the Japanese for six years, the United States National Women's Team began a serious attempt to copy their serving technique during practice for the 1970 World Volleyball Championships in Bulgaria.

In 1969 a Japanese student, Toshi Toyoda, arrived in the United States to study and play volleyball at UCLA. He came with a mastery of the round house floater serve and was the most effective server in the 1969 and 1970 USVBA National Championships. In 1969 he was one of the few men at the USVBA Championships to use the round house floater; in 1970 there were a few more players who had begun to use the round house floater but had not yet perfected it.

The round house floater serve is currently the most effective serve to be used in local, regional and national competition, because of its unique dropping and side-to-side movement. Few players in the United States have mastered this serve; therefore, there has been little opportunity for practice in receiving it.

Better players were reluctant to try a new serving style because they would have had to endure a temporary loss of serving effectiveness while they were struggling to learn the new technique. Until the round house floater serve becomes common in this country, it will remain the most effective serve in local, regional and national competition. Because it can be hit with great force, with a dropping side-to-side movement that has proven unpredictable to receivers, more players will soon be using this technique.

To accomplish the round house serve, the player stands with his shoulders perpendicular to the net, feet shoulder-width apart and knees slightly flexed. He tosses the ball about 3 ft. in the air, slightly in front of and above his forward shoulder. During the toss, his body leans backward as both legs bend. His hitting arm swings upward from the area of his right knee in a fully extended windmill motion. As the ball starts to descend, he shifts his weight forward and extends his legs. He contacts the ball with the *heel* of his hand, directly above the right shoulder. (If the ball is contacted *behind* the shoulder, it usually has a high trajectory and travels out of the opponents' court. If the ball is contacted *in front of* the shoulder, it usually travels in a very low trajectory and hits the net.)

The weight of the player's body should be supported by his front leg when the ball is hit. After contact the server pivots on his front foot and faces the net, ready to move to his defensive assignment.

Round house spin serve

The round house spin serve is used by many male members of powerful European teams. It is a very fast serve which drops rapidly but cannot be directed with the same accuracy as floater serves. Once the ball leaves the server's hands, the receivers can predict its flight; thus, members of our National Men's Teams have enjoyed passing this serve and have not attempted to copy the European serving techniques.

The outstanding difference between the technical execution of the round house spin serve and the round house floater is in contacting the ball with the striking hand. For the spin serve the ball is struck with the entire cupped hand in the same manner as for the overhand spin serve. Although the hand can be held open for the floater serve, contact is made with the heel of the hand.

a   b   c

d   e

Fig. 2.7 Round House Floater Serve *All American Toshi Toyoda prefers to move far behind the end line so that he can contact the ball with great force and still direct it into his opponents' court. (Ealing Corp.)*

SERVING DRILLS

Serving practice should be held at the beginning, middle and end of practice sessions to simulate game conditions when players are fresh, tired or exhausted.

To allow the server to see where each serve lands, the court should be cleared of receivers and the players divided along the end lines of the available courts so they can serve back and forth across the net. When the ball lands out of bounds, the player recovering the serve should signal how far the ball was out to allow the server to adjust the force or direction of the serve. The server should always serve from the serving area behind the right third of the court, unless practicing a straight-ahead or line serve. When practicing line serves, each player might have a partner who stands on the opposite side of the net serving the ball back and forth from any position behind the end line.

Since serving is probably the dullest fundamental to practice, it is best to make the drills competitive by placing towels, chairs or other markers on the floor for players to hit. The coach may want to keep a practice serving chart to record the players' scores. It is important that players do not "ease up" when using targets but deliver their toughest serves during all drills.

It is often beneficial to combine serving and receiving drills, since each player should receive from 50 to 100 serves during every practice session. If the drill is server-orientated, the receiver can be placed in position at the discretion of the server. For example, if the server wishes to serve cross court, the receiver takes the right front or right back position.

A simple game can provide motivation between two players by letting the receiver score one point each time the ball is passed to a designated target area, and giving a point to the server each time the receiver fails to pass the ball accurately. Balls that are served out, into the net or away from the receiver's area are scored for the receiver.

Another server-receiving game incorporates some of the pressure inherent during actual competition. To win this game, either the server or the serve receiver must score 3 straight points. For example, if the server has 2 points and the receiver has passed the ball perfectly, the receiver takes the lead, 1 to 0. As soon as the opponent scores, the other player's score automatically returns to 0.

A third player can be added to act as the passing target for the receiver. When one of the players wins, the third player exchanges positions with the winner and the loser remains in the same position. In this manner the weakest player gets the added work that is needed to improve performance. It is surprising how readily a coach can detect which performers will do well in pressure situations from such a simple game.

The most time-consuming but effective way for the server to practice is to direct serves against the type of live team-receiving formation that will be faced in competition. Weaknesses inherent in the formation can be pointed out to the server, and those weak points can be attacked. For a detailed analysis of serving strategy, see the section on Team Play (pages 161–210).

3

The Pass

THE PASS

The *pass* is the reception of the serve or first contact of the ball by the offense. It is an attempt to control the movement of the ball to another player who hits it into the air or "sets" the ball in position for a teammate to attack the ball from above the level of the net into the opponents' court. Occasionally, the pass is attacked to confuse the opponents' block. The passer in highly competitive or "power" volleyball should attempt to receive the serve in an underhand manner; the intention is one of striking the ball with both forearms simultaneously.

Overhand pass

The overhand pass is not recommended for receiving serves in power volleyball because players who use this method are frequently called for illegal hits. In 1966 a total of 1,500 serve receptions were charted at the USVBA National Championships in Grand Rapids, Michigan. Ninety-six percent of these serves were played with the forearm pass, 4 percent with the overhand pass. The referees called 30 percent of the overhand receptions illegal hits.[1] Since 1966, an even greater percentage of serve receptions in USVBA competition have been played with the forearm pass.

Players in the front line stand 15 ft. or more from the net to receive the serve. If the ball is above their waist, they usually let the ball travel to a backcourt player. The backcourt players stand deep in their court so that any ball above their waist will travel past the back line and out of bounds.

Fig. 3.1 Overhand Pass
The player faces the direction of the intended target area and forms a cup with her fingers to contact the ball directly in front of her face. Her back is slightly arched, and she follows through in a synchronized movement of legs, body and arms. (Dr. Leonard Stallcup)

Forearm Pass

At one time the forearm pass was only used to receive serves by players who had "bad hands" and did not want to risk a rule infraction, or by players who were not in a position to use the overhand pass. The restrictions placed on the serving area,* removal of the serving screen and new techniques of the forearm pass have enabled players to pass the ball with better accuracy than the overhand method. In fact, recent directives from the International Volleyball Federation and United States Volleyball Association encouraging the return of the overhand pass have gone unheeded by players and coaches.

The forearm pass is also used to handle low balls and spikes. When used to recover the opponents' attack it is called a *dig*. Up to 50 percent of a team's practice can be devoted to this fundamental. (The defensive technique of digging will be covered in Chapter 11 along with the *dive* and *roll*.)

HAND POSITION

The ball *must not* be played with the open palms in the underhand position, or else the referee will call a foul. There is no written rule prohibiting the use of the open hand in underhand play, but the universal interpretation of officials is that the ball cannot be clearly hit using this technique.

---

* The serving area is 10 ft. wide and in the right third of the server's court.

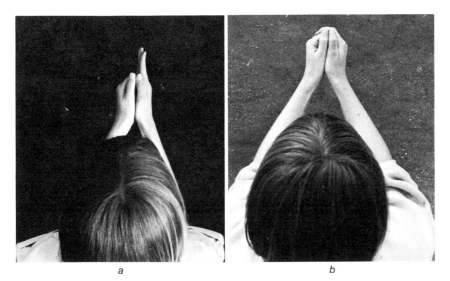

a   b

Fig. 3.2 Clenched Fist *Fist is clenched, thumb on top of index finger. Place thumbs parallel and wrap fingers around closed fist. This is the most popular method. (Lurline K. Fujii)*

The hands should be clasped in a manner that is comfortable and effective for the individual player. Experience has shown that beginning players can readily learn the popular *clenched-fist* position. This hand position presents a good rebounding service for balls that cannot be reached with the forearms and must be struck with the hands.

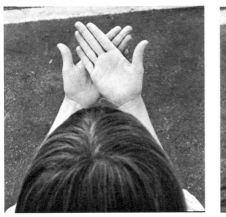

a   b

Fig. 3.3 Curled Fingers *Hands are held open, one hand over the other (a). Fingers are curled and thumbs parallel to create a flat surface (b). (Lurline K. Fujii)*

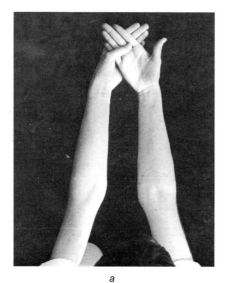
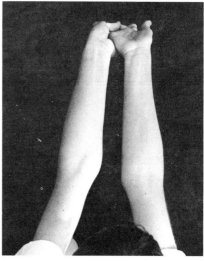

a   b

Fig. 3.4 Thumb over Palm   *The thumb of the bottom hand is folded over the top hand. Hands are pointed toward the floor to rotate the forearms outward, and to create a flat rebounding surface. If the ball is contacted by the hands in this position, rather than the forearms, the referee may call a thrown ball. (Lurline K. Fujii)*

The *curled fingers* position allows more of an outward rotation of the forearms.

The *thumb-over-palm* position allows the player to achieve a maximum outward rotation of his forearms, which creates a very favorable flat rebounding service. This position should not be used by most men since their wide shoulder structure usually prevents them from bringing their forearms close together to form a favorable rebounding surface.

ARM POSITION

At the 1956 World Games in Paris, the American team displayed good control with the "bump" pass. Other national teams preferred to squat low or roll to the floor in using the overhand pass, and only "bumped" the serve when it was impossible to use the overhand method.

About 1960, the Japanese women began receiving the serve on their wrists and forearms with amazing accuracy. They would keep their elbows locked upon contact. Within a few years all countries began to utilize the new techniques of the forearm pass.

In the early 1960's the term "bump" was still used to describe all serves passed in the underhand manner. By 1965 most of the players contacted the ball on their forearms instead of with wrists and hands.

The most popular method of forearm passing is called the *elbow lock*.

Fig. 3.5 "Bump" Pass (old style) *The ball is contacted with clasped hands; elbows are bent. (Dr. Leonard Stallcup)*

Fig. 3.6 Forearm Pass (modern) *Strict interpretation of a thrown ball during overhand serve reception forces almost total reliance on the forearm pass. The greater area of the forearms enables the receiver to misjudge the flight of the ball by 3 or 4 in. and still make an accurate pass. (Los Angeles City Unified School District)*

a b

Fig. 3.7 Contact Area *Some players are flexible enough to create an ideal rebounding surface from their wrists to elbows (a). Others must be satisfied to extend their arms close together and contact the ball on the lower forearm or wrist (b). (Los Angeles City Unified School District)*

a b

Fig. 3.8 Elbow Lock *Upward coordinated movement of legs and arms is important when the ball is moving slowly. There should be little forward body or arm movement when receiving fast serves, or the pass will travel too far. The ball should contact both forearms simultaneously. (Ealing Corp.)*

Arms remain locked before and during contact. Movement of the arms is directed in an arc from the shoulders.

The newer passing technique is called the *elbow snap*. Before contact the arms are held in a relaxed manner, elbows bent. Just before contact, elbows are extended and wrists and forearms are brought close together. On a fast serve the elbow snap technique requires considerably less leg action because the arms move very quickly as they snap forward to contact the ball. This technique is relatively new and gaining in popularity.

a   b

Fig. 3.9 Elbow Snap *When low fast passes are desired, the elbow snap is recommended. The coordinated leg-and-arm action shown is used when passing slow-moving balls. (Los Angeles City Unified School District)*

In both the elbow lock and elbow snap, hands should be clasped together, thumbs parallel. Prior to contact, elbows should be completely extended and rotated outward exposing the flat inner surface of the forearms. Thumbs and wrists should be pointed toward the floor, and the ball should contact the internal part of the forearms *above* the wrist. The speed and movement of the arms depend on the speed of the approaching ball and the distance the pass must travel.

PASSING TECHNIQUES

Successful serve receivers anticipate the flight of the ball and quickly position their body in its path before contact. The body is lowered or raised so that the ball can be contacted slightly above the waist. The receiver leans slightly forward, back straight and arms fully extended, elbows rotated outward to form a flat rebound surface with the forearms. The player watches the ball before, during and after contact.

Fig. 3.10 Passing the Serve *Feet are shoulder-width apart and can vary from a perpendicular to stride position. Knees are bent and the trunk is inclined forward. The passer moves directly in front of the ball and will make contact waist-high in the center of her body. (Bud Fields)*

Follow-through of the arms and knees depends on the speed of the approaching serve and intended placement of the ball. If the ball moves over the net slowly, or must be passed a long distance, the player's arms and legs should move upward as contact is made; this gives greater impetus to the flight of the ball.

Generally, hard overhand floater serves require little follow-through. A hard overhand or round house spin serve requires no follow-through at all. In fact, front row receivers often "cushion" a hard spin serve by leaning back when the ball is contacted, thus preventing the pass from rebounding

a   b

Fig. 3.11 Passing the Low Serve *The technique for passing a low serve is mastered by players who can perform a half- (a) to full squat (b) with good body control. If the player is not under the ball, contact may be made with thumbs and wrists instead of forearms (a). (Bud Fields, a; Dr. Leonard Stallcup, b)*

Fig. 3.12 Japanese Technique *The pass travels in a fast, low arc. To achieve a low trajectory, the ball is contacted with arms pointing toward the floor, back held straight. (Dr. Leonard Stallcup)*

over the net. Squatting must be practiced. (American players naturally react to low balls by lowering themselves from the waist instead of lowering their bodies with their legs, as is the custom of the Asians and Europeans.)

The Japanese teams use the fastest offense in volleyball. They have developed a quick, low pass that gets to the setter before the opposing blockers have a chance to observe the attack patterns of the spikers. The Japanese consider the pass to be the most important part of the offense and spend over 50 percent of their practice time passing serves and spikes. Instead of passing the ball up above the net, they concentrate on passing in a low trajectory, into the path of the oncoming setter. This pass is particularly advantageous to a fast three-hitter attack.

MOVING TO THE BALL

Correct body position greatly enhances the likelihood of an accurate pass. After moving to the desired depth in the court, a lateral slide step positions the player behind the ball. Since players have a relatively long time to react to the approaching serve, the *slide step* should move the player behind the ball before the serve arrives. The slide step is exactly the same as the defensive step in basketball in that the legs are never crossed. This technique allows the receiver to keep his head and body facing the oncoming ball while he quickly shifts his position.

The first step is initiated by taking a long sideway stride with the inside foot; then the outside foot moves alongside the other foot and the movements are repeated until the desired position is reached. Due to the unpredictable action of the floater serve, a last split-second adjustment is sometimes necessary.

Fig. 3.13 Lining Up the Ball   *The player moves the upper part of his body behind the ball by taking a long slide step and squatting to the height of the ball on the same leg while extending the other leg. (Ealing Corp.)*

Fig. 3.14 Screw Under Step *The passer has executed a screw under step to position the upper part of her body behind the ball just prior to contact. Beginners rarely make this split-second adjustment and usually rely on a lateral arm movement to compensate for poor body position. (Bud Fields)*

a

b

c

Fig. 3.15 Changing Direction *This player has been instructed to keep her hands clasped close to her body before initiating arm movement. This is desirable when using the elbow snap technique. (Lurline K. Fujii)*

a

b

c

Fig. 3.16 Changing Direction *Changing direction with the elbow lock technique is recommended for providing greater control and to enable the forearms to remain in contact with the ball for a longer period of time. Prolonged contact is maintained by lateral rotation of the body and arms. (Ealing Corp.)*

If the ball suddenly breaks to one side, the receiver may position his body behind the ball by taking a long slide step and squatting on the same leg while extending the other leg. This maneuver has become commonly known as the *screw under step* for lack of a more descriptive term.

CHANGING DIRECTION

When time does not allow the passer to face the intended target, his body, head and arms should pivot toward the target area as the ball is being passed. The technique shown in Fig. 3.15 is excellent for beginners because it prevents them from swinging vigorously at the ball and hitting it with too much force. Changing direction with the elbow snap is difficult, however, because there is little opportunity for the body and arm rotation necessary for prolonged contact with the ball.

LATERAL PASS

The passer must reach laterally to contact the ball when there is not enough time to position his body for the regular forearm pass. When both arms are used, this technique is called a *lateral pass*.

Fig. 3.17 Low Lateral Pass *In the lateral pass, the inside shoulder dips forward to turn the interior part of the forearms toward the ball. The player leans toward the ball in a lateral tilt, weight over his front leg.*

a

b

Fig. 3.18 High Lateral Pass   *Often players must extend their legs completely or jump to orient the interior part of their forearms toward the ball when passing at shoulder height. (Bob Van Wagner, a; Dr. Leonard Stallcup, b)*

Fig. 3.19 Lateral Pass   *(common error) This player did not sufficiently dip his inside shoulder; consequently, the ball has skidded off his arms and is rebounding backward. (Dr. Leonard Stallcup)*

ONE-ARM PASS

When the ball is too far away to contact with the lateral pass, a one-arm pass, or dig, is used. Volleyball lore tells us that the term *dig* originated from beach play: Players would scoop low balls inches from the sand, using their fists and a bent elbow. Today, most players use the forearm to contact the ball whenever possible. The fist is used on balls that are harder to reach.

Fig. 3.20   One-Arm Pass   *The one-arm pass is frequently used in competition and often overlooked in practice. Contact can be made with the forearm, wrist or fist. (Bud Fields)*

BACKWARD PASS

The backward pass is often used by a backcourt player to recover balls hit off the top of the blocker's hands. Occasionally, players amaze their teammates by making perfect sets from the back line area or further with this technique.

The elbow lock technique shown in Fig. 3.21 is recommended for hitting the ball with enough power to reach the net at distances of 30 ft. or more. On closer plays, the player rarely must turn his back and run the ball down.

Fig. 3.21 Backward Pass *Just before contact, shoulders shrug upward and the player leans backward. (Dr. Leonard Stallcup)*

UNEXPECTED POSITIONS

During the game the player will often be called on to pass the ball from unusual positions. Players who have been thoroughly drilled to react to the ball do not hesitate to place themselves in whatever position necessary to pass the ball. To prevent injury the player must faithfully stretch muscles; to meet the demands of competition he must maintain the proper flexibility.

Fig. 3.22 Passing a Dink Shot *The player drops beyond a full squatting position to field a dink shot looped behind the blockers. (Bud Fields)*

REFERENCE

1. Robins, Janis. A statistical comparison, Duluth '61-Grand Rapids 66. In *International Volleyball Review*, April-May, 1967, p. 46.

4

The Set

The *set* is an overhand or forearm pass that places the ball in position for one of the spikers to attack it. The set is usually performed by a special-ist called the *setter*, who uses the overhand pass whenever possible. The *overhand pass* is a more precise method of delivering the set and it gives the

a   *b*

Fig. 4.1 Basic Position   *The setter is positioned directly in front of the ball, hands held about 6 in. in front of the face (a). Unless the ball is contacted simultaneously with fingers and thumbs of both hands (b), it may be called a foul. (Bud Fields, a; Los Angeles City Unified School District, b)*

Fig. 4.2 Set *Ernie Suwara, Outstanding Athlete of the 1964 United States Olympic Trials, delivers a back set to approaching spiker, Larry Rundle. Rundle was named Most Valuable Player in the 1968,1969,1970 National Open Championships.*

spiker a better opportunity to analyze the flight of the approaching ball. The overhand pass utilizes the fingertips of both hands to contact the ball. If the ball has not been clearly hit or has not visibly come to rest, the setter has committed an error.

The usual offense employs two setters and four spikers. Beginning setters need superior speed, mobility and anticipation to move quickly under the pass and deliver a *normal set* in a high arc that drops about 2 ft. from the net at either corner of the net.

Good setters require superior reactions and ball handling skills so that they can place the ball at any spot along the net at any height. Better setters possess the mental alertness and control to take advantage of the blocker's weaknesses and their spikers' strengths. They know the individual preferences of their spikers and are capable of watching the spiker's approach, ball and opposing blockers when positioning themselves to receive a good pass. They have the competitive spirit to bolster their teammates' play and perform well in clutch situations.

FRONT SET

When the ball is passed, the setter must anticipate its flight and move quickly under it; he must be in a stationary, relaxed position when the ball arrives. His feet should be in a stride position, shoulder-width apart. The foot closest to the net should remain flat on the floor until contact. The forward foot should be pointed in the direction of the set. The setter's nose should be in line with the descending ball, and his hands should be cupped about 6 in. in front of his face prior to contact.

a   b   c

Fig. 4.3 Front Set *The ball's force has caused the player's fingers to bend backward and come within 3 or 4 in. of his face (a). Index and forefingers supply most of the force as fingers and wrist spring forward (b). Smooth follow-through helps to insure a well-directed pass (c). (Ealing Corp.)*

Beginners should be coached to "form a window" in front of the face. When the ball is about to be contacted, weight shifts over the front foot and the back foot rests on the toes. The setter should be directly behind the ball, elbows close to the sides of his body and upper arms horizontal to the floor. His hands should be held approximately 6 in. in front of his head, wrists cocked and fingers spread. He contacts the ball with his fingertips and second joint of the thumb, index and middle fingers, and extends his entire body in a synchronized movement.

a

b

c

Fig. 4.4 Setting a Low Pass *The player's buttocks are close to the floor and hands are in front of his face. Back is straight at contact and weight is centered behind the back foot. He follows through with his arms as he drops to the floor.* (Ealing Corp.)

d

e

BACK SET

The back set is used to confuse the block. For this reason the setter must be careful not to arch his back too soon, or else experienced middle blockers will "read" the play and get an early jump on the ball. The back set utilizes the same initial body position as the front set. The hands contact the ball above the forehead and extend up as the back arches. The head should be kept up as the arms follow through.

a   *b*   *c*

Fig. 4.5 Back Set *Contact is made above the forehead with the palms remaining up and back throughout the release and follow-through. Patti Bright delivers the back set.* (Los Angeles City Unified School District)

LATERAL SET

The lateral set should be attempted in game conditions by superior ball handlers only. Average setters should stay with the safe strategy of facing the direction they intend to set and use an occasional back set to confuse the blocker. Generally, referees on the local level carefully scrutinize the lateral set, which is a relatively new technique developed to complement three-hitter offenses.

Some outstanding Japanese and East European setters prefer to receive passes with their backs to the net and deliver their sets laterally for greater deception. This technique allows the setter to keep his fingers on the ball for a greater period of time; consequently, the ball is placed with greater accuracy.

At this time, referees from other countries in the FIVB, unlike United States National Referees, are more liberal in their interpretations of what constitutes a legal set. At the USVBA Championships there are still some referees who insist that the setter release the ball with a flick of his wrist and fingers, directly forward or opposite the direction he is facing. Successful setters are flexible enough to adapt their style to the philosophy of the referee on the stand. Generally, referees of regional and national status on the West Coast are allowing setters to use the lateral sets, which make the three-hitter attack function so effectively. The majority of referees in the rest of the country, however, prefer the traditional front-and-back setting style, which favors relatively limited contact of the fingers on the ball.

Traditionalists argue that we in the United States invented the game and do not have to change our interpretations merely to conform to the tainted throwing style of setting used by the most successful teams in world competition. Players on national USA teams and American referees of international stature point to the handicaps that American teams face in international

Fig. 4.6 Lateral Set *Movement of the arms is to the side rather than forward or backward. Larry Griebenow, Outstanding Male Rookie of 1970, is shown delivering the set to his left at the National Championship Tournament in Hawaii. (Dr. Leonard Stallcup)*

competition when opposing setters, who have mastered the lateral sets, cause American blockers to miss assignments. Setters representing the United States have been taught the predictable forward-and-back style of setting which international blockers enjoy.

TRADITIONAL SETTING POSITION

The pass is directed to a designated target area about 2–4 ft. from the net. This area is usually the middle of the court in the two-hitter attack and 10 ft. from the passers' right side line in the three-hitter attack. The instant the server contacts the ball, the setter should move toward the designated target area, while watching the serve receiver, to anticipate the flight of the pass.

In Fig. 4.7, Larry Rundle takes a long squatting step to the side with his right leg while he extends his left. He lowers his body until his face is even with the ball's height (*a*). He quickly pivots on his right foot as he releases the ball to the left so that his body, head and arms are turned in the direction of the ball's flight (*b*). He extends his arms, wrists and fingers as he falls toward the floor. After the set, his squatting leg remains flexed; buttocks and lower and upper back touch the floor. When his shoulder blades touch the floor, the player rocks forward and regains a standing position.

a   *b*

Fig. 4.7 Low Lateral Set   *The low lateral set is difficult because the player must pivot quickly on his squatting leg until his body faces the direction of the set.* (Ealing Corp.)

If the pass is good, the traditional strategy is for the setter to position his body, side toward the net, knees bent and hands up—thus forming a window in front of his face. As the ball travels across the center of the body, contact occurs about 6 in. in front of his eyes. The setter moves in the direction of the set to "back up" the spiker in the event the spike is blocked.

When the pass is short of the target area, the setter must hurry to get

Fig. 4.8 Good Tactical Setting Positic
When the setter positions her body, face an
arms in a direct line with the approaching ba
the opposing blockers have no clue as to th
intended direction of the set. (Los Angel€
City Unified School District)

Fig. 4.9 Poor Tactical Setting Position
This occurs when the setter can deliver the
ball in one direction only. Patti Bright's tech-
nique is flawless as she steps behind the ball
and faces in the direction of her front set.
(Los Angeles City Unified School District)

behind the ball so the set will not have to be made on the run. Traditional strategy calls for the setter to face the corner of the net where the set will be delivered. Of course, two blockers will probably be waiting at that point before the setter touches the ball. Better setters learn to set the ball laterally to the other side of the net if the middle blocker leaves early in anticipation of a normal set.

Most beginners make a mistake when setting the type of pass shown in Fig. 4.9. They try to set this kind of pass on the run instead of actually stopping slightly beyond the ball, thereby allowing contact to be made in a direct line between setter and target area. (Notice how Patti Bright has followed through, extended her arms and legs, to insure the proper height and distance of the set.)

The *jump set* is used to place the setter in position to save a long pass that will drop over or hit the net. It is also a means of confusing the block. Better front court setters in the two-hitter attack may jump in the air and decide to spike or set the ball according to the reaction of the opposing block. If the blockers remain on the ground, the setter gets a free spike; if the blocker or blockers jump with the setter, they cannot react fast enough to chase the set to another attacker. Back row setters in the three-hitter attack use the jump set to confuse inexperienced blockers, even though they cannot spike unless they take off from behind the 10-ft. line.

STRATEGY

Setters should decide what type of setting strategy will best work against their opponents. They should know who are the strongest and weakest blockers on the opposing team, and observe their blocking switches in the event that the strategy calls for continual setting in front of the weaker blocker. When the opposition is in the habit of stacking its strongest blockers on the star spiker, it may be advisable to set a less capable spiker against a weaker block.

Setters should be familiar with the referee's style as well as their opponents'. Although the same USVBA rules are in effect in all USVBA, NCAA, NAIA, AAU and other major organizational play, interpretation of those rules may vary considerably from one referee to another. Usually, the average setter is not overly concerned with the referee's interpretation of a thrown ball, since most of his sets are of the high and wide variety and are delivered in the traditional manner. Better players, who are capable of setting in a three-attack and have become used to delivering the ball from a variety of body positions, are very concerned.

Better setters can cause blockers to move in the wrong direction or move too late to block effectively. Some of the techniques used include faking a back set by stepping backward and arching the back, thereby contacting the ball high above the forehead and delivering a front set. The opposite ploy is to step forward without arching the back and deliver a back set.

Fig. 4.10 Saving a Long Pass *All American Dane Holtzman leaps in the air to prevent a high pass from traveling into the net. Contact is about to be made above his forehead; his arched back indicates a back set.*

a   b

Fig. 4.11 Confusing the Block *Larry Rundle draws the blocker on a ball passed close to the net. The ball is set from in front of the face in the usual manner. The blocker cannot touch the set unless an obvious attempt is made by the setter to score a point or side out. (Ealing Corp.)*

The latest technique is to wait for the pass with the back to the net and set the ball laterally.

When beginners use these techniques, it is called bad form and a poor grasp of the fundamentals of setting. When expert setters use them and deliver the set cleanly and accurately, they are classified as players with an exciting and innovative style.

Fig. 4.12 Setting a Blocked Ball
Toshi Toyoda sets a blocked ball from the off-blocker position. One knee touches the floor. Toshi lowers his body so that he can contact the ball directly in front of his face. (Ealing Corp.)

Recently, a very talented setter who had developed the style described above, lost an important match for his team in the USVBA National Championships because he would not deliver the ball in the traditional manner demanded by the referee—that is, from in front of his face in the direction he was facing or directly opposite the way he was facing. He often set the ball laterally with his back to the net. His team would have won handily if he would have delivered a normal set and let his spikers provide the deception necessary to defeat the block by varying the spike. Deception is a good goal for the setter and worth striving for, but he must be flexible enough to evaluate quickly the limits the referee establishes for him and change his style if necessary.

Sets from the right back should normally be delivered in a high arc to the left front of the court, as shown in Fig. 4.13. Smaller players may have to

Fig. 4.13 Setting from the Right Back *The left front spiker (No. 10) is the only player who can watch the flight of the ball while using a proper approach to attack the set.* (Ealing Corp.)

squat halfway to the floor and extend their legs in a synchronized motion upon contact to insure the necessary height and distance for this type of set.

TEACHING PROGRESSION

The following teaching progression has been used successfully with secondary school players.

1. Demonstrate the hand position for the overhand set. Instruct the players to form a window with their hands, 6 in. in front of the face, fingers spread and elbows close to the body. Check each member of the group individually.

2. Divide the group into partners and have them face each other at a distance of 5 ft. Pass out one slightly underinflated leather volleyball for every two people. Assign one partner as a tosser and the other as a volleyer. From a distance of 5 ft., demonstrate a two-hand underhand toss that falls in an arc on your partner's forehead. Instruct the volleyers

to return the ball in an arc that will land on the tosser's forehead. Stress contacting the ball with the fingertips. After 10 tosses, partners should exchange roles. To provide motivation, the volleyer scores one point everytime the pass drops in an arc over the tosser's head. The first partner to score 15 points wins.

3. Demonstrate a three-quarter squat, back held straight, and simulate an overhand pass. Stress keeping the "window" in front of the face. Have the class squat and simulate a pass with you while you verbally correct individual form. Repeat drill number 2 above, using a low underhand toss that drops at the waist.

4. Demonstrate a slide step with the outside foot, and pivot on both feet to face the tosser. Instruct the tossers to lob the ball from side to side to make the volleyers take a lateral step to get behind the ball. Stress the pivot so the volleyer is facing in the direction of the set. Increase the difficulty by instructing the tosser to lob the ball so that the volleyer must take two slide steps before pivoting.

5. Demonstrate the technique for setting a low pass to either side. Take a long slide step and squat on the same leg to the level of the toss while fully extending the other leg. Body weight is over the squatting leg. Body, head and arms turn toward the tosser and simulate a set. Turn your back to the class and instruct them to move with you. Check individual form and then give each partner ten tosses before changing roles. Stress the pivot and turn toward the tosser.

6. Instruct the partners to rally from a distance of 5 ft. Use all of the techniques in the preceding drills 2-5 to keep the ball in play.

7. Increase the distance between partners to 10 ft. Show the class how to bend their legs and extend them to gain additional power and distance in the set. Instruct the tosser to lob the ball in an arc that falls near the volleyer's head. Change roles after ten tosses. Stress keeping the hands 6 in. in front of the face. Power is lost when contact is made with extended arms.

8. Instruct the partners to rally from a sitting position at a distance of 5 ft. Stress moving the upper part of the body behind the ball by leaning laterally. Point out how difficult it is to set the ball when hands are not in front of the face.

9. Move partners to a standing position, 10 ft. apart. Instruct the tosser to lob the ball in a high arc anywhere within a 5-ft. radius of the volleyer. The volleyer must move quickly to get under the ball and face the setter before contacting the ball.

10. Divide the players into groups of three. Place them in a straight line at a distance of 5 ft. apart. Demonstrate the back set. Have the class simulate a back set. Stress contacting the ball above the forehead and arching the back. Follow through with hands above the head. Tossers on the end lob the ball to the middle player, who back sets it to the other tosser. The volleyer turns and repeats the drill. Rotate after

ten back sets. Increase the distance between players to 10 ft. and repeat.

11. After players learn the rudiments of the back set, they can be paired off once again and placed 10 ft. apart. Demonstrate how to set the ball about 5 ft. straight overhead, and quickly make a half-turn and back set the ball to your partner. He sets the ball overhead, pivots and returns the back set. Stress a quick pivot and stationary body position before setting.

12. Demonstrate the lateral set. Pass the ball about 5 ft. overhead, execute a quarter-turn and set the ball laterally to your partner, who will pass directly above the head, make a quarter-turn and deliver a lateral set back to you. Stress moving arms and body to the side as the ball is set.

Setting with One Ball to Two Players *Start by overhand passing back and forth in a straight line.*

Partners face each other in a straight line, shoulders at a right angle to the set. They set back and forth from a distance of 15 ft. As they warm up, the distance increases to 30 ft. Setting specialists should always drill by the net.

Return to the 15-ft. distance and set the ball laterally. Players drilling by the net should stand facing the net. Halfway through this drill, partners should change positions to practice setting to the left and right. Gradually increase this distance.

SETTER   SETTER

Partners once again stand facing each other, shoulders at a right angle to the net. They pass the ball 5-10 ft. directly overhead, turn halfway around so that their back is toward their partner and set backwards. The partner passes to himself and returns the back set. Gradually increase the distance to 30 ft.

Partners stand about 10 ft. apart. The tosser lobs the ball from knee- to waist-high directly at the setter. The setter squats and delivers a 15-ft. set that drops in the area of the tosser's head. Increase the distance between partners.

The tosser lobs the ball from side to side at a distance of 10 ft. The setter takes short fast slide steps to reach the area of the toss; then, he takes a long lateral step and squats on the outside leg, pivots and sets to the tosser.

Cross Court Set—Three Players *Balls set from the backcourt should travel cross court so that the spiker can watch the approaching set. The setter starts in any standard backcourt defensive position the team uses. The middle back position is a good one to drill from, since this area usually receives many balls that are deflected by the block. One of the spikers lobs balls to the backcourt, and the setter delivers the ball cross court. The spiker who receives the set can also practice by setting to the other spiker.*

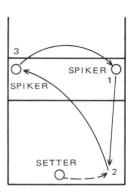

Setting on the Run *Although every setter should strive to contact the ball with his feet in a stationary position, a great number of sets, made on the run, are necessary. The following drill should be introduced during the first week of practice before poor techniques of setting on the run can be developed. The coach lobs the ball 10-15 ft. in front of the setter so that the player can just manage to contact the ball using the overhand passing technique. If the setter is close to the spiker, he attempts to set the ball straight up in the air. The forward momentum of the setter's body will cause the ball to travel in a forward arc. The great majority of sets delivered on the run travel too far because the setter attempts to set the ball forward.*

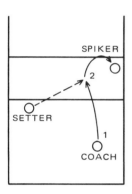

Cross Court Set—Four Players *When four players are used in the cross court setting drill, the ball is kept in continuous motion with the overhand pass.*

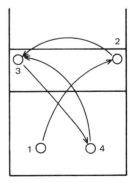

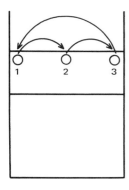

Back Set *Although most coaches prefer their spikers to set the ball in front of them there are always situations that demand a back set. One player works on a 15-ft. set, the middle player on a back set and the other player on a 30-ft. set. Rotate to all positions.*

Long and Short Back Sets *The middle player delivers a back set from both directions. The setter can vary the distance between the spikers to practice back sets of varying heights and distances.*

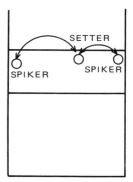

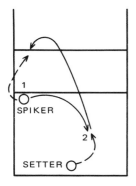

Backcourt Set and Spike *The spiker tosses the ball over his shoulder to the setter in the backcourt and approaches for the spike. A blocker or blockers may be added.*

Dig and Set *The coach stands on a table and spikes the ball at either of the two backcourt players. The player who does not dig the ball must set it to one of the two spikers stationed at the corners of the net.*

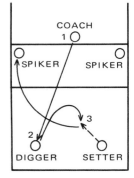

Decision Set *This is a drill for advanced players. Three spikers start 10-12 ft. from the net and attack against three blockers. The object of the drill is to spike the ball against one blocker or no block. One spiker sets a teammate; if a two-man block forms in front of the spiker who has received the set, he must set one of his two teammates. If a spiker receives the second set, he must hit it over the net. This drill is very beneficial if spikers are learning the jump set. It can also be used with two attackers against three blockers.*

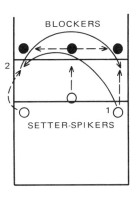

FOR SETTING SPECIALISTS

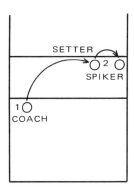

Short Back Set *Anytime a setting specialist is having difficulty with a particular set, the coach should develop a drill to solve the problem. The setter in the three-hitter attack should receive the set about 10 ft. from the right side line and face the two on-hand spikers. The setter often neglects the spiker approaching down the right side line and needs extra practice on the short back set. The coach should pass balls to the setter from various positions on the court and evaluate the placement of each set. After the setter releases the ball, he must quickly turn and cover the spiker to field spikes that rebound off the block.*

Jump Set *Setters who master the jump set can greatly improve the effectiveness of their attack. The coach should attempt to lob balls 1 or 2 ft. over the net as the setter runs in from various court positions and attempts to "save" the pass by reaching above the net and setting the ball before it crosses the tape. Instruct the spiker to stand at various attack positions along the net.*

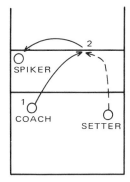

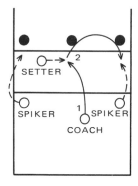

Spike or Set When the front court setter approaches a high pass that is close to the net on the on-hand side, he can often spike the ball without any blocker opposing him. Often, blockers are concentrating on the spikers and do not expect the setter to spike on second contact with the ball. Better setters can jump in the air and, depending on the reaction of the opposing blocker, set or spike the ball. The coach should vary the height and distance of the pass. After the setter learns the fundamental technique of the jump set, the drill should be run against aggressive blockers.

Move Backward and Front Set Most setters deliver a back set when they take several steps backward to line up the ball. This is particularly true when they are close to the side line. They must learn to deliver a front set under these conditions, with enough distance and height to reach the spiker on the other side of court. The coach should pass the ball behind the spiker from various positions on the court and instruct the setter to deliver a front set.

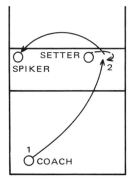

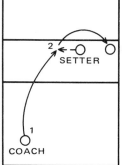

Move Forward and Back Set Most setters are in the habit of setting forward when they run forward to line up the pass. Pass the ball well in front of the setter from various court positions and instruct the setter to deliver a back set.

Lateral Set When a setter must run behind the 10-ft. line to line up the pass, he can generally set the ball only in the direction he is facing. Good ball handlers can be taught to set laterally, however. The threat of a lateral set is important because it will force the middle blocker to stay "honest" and remain in the center of the court until the setter releases the ball. The coach passes the ball around the 10-ft. line from various areas of the court and instructs the setter to set laterally.

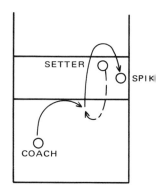

Lateral Set Facing the Net *When a low pass drops close to the net, the average setter must play the ball with the forearm pass. A setter with "good hands" can be taught to squat and face the net to set the ball laterally for best accuracy. The coach lobs low passes at various locations along the net.*

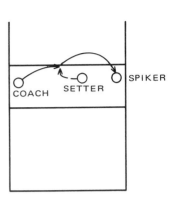

Lateral Set with the Back Toward the Net *The setter in the three-hitter attack must learn the lateral set, or the middle spiker will only receive the ball on a perfect pass. Pass the ball from various areas of the court while moving the setter off the net to force a lateral set to the middle attacker.*

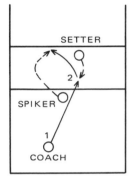

Backcourt Dig and Set *The simplest play for the middle in player to make is a set to the corner spiker whom he is facing. The coach stands on a table and spikes to a backcourt digger. The middle in player runs under the dig and delivers a front set to the end spiker.*

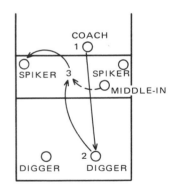

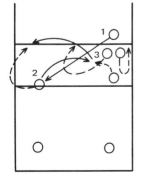

Dig and Set *The next step is to allow the middle in player to set any of the attackers.*

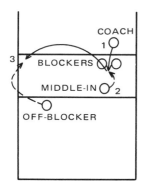

Middle In Sets to Off-Blocker   The middle in player has numerous opportunities to set balls looped over or deflected by the block. Often the only attacker who can get in position to spike on the quick change to offense is the former off-blocker. The coach stands on a table and dinks over the blockers. The middle in player sets the dink to the off-blocker.

Setting the Attack   The setter must be familiar with the idiosyncrasies of the spikers he will be playing next to in actual competition. Long hours of practice are necessary to refine the attack that has been selected. Teams that use the middle in defense must give extra setting practice to the players covering the area behind the block. This player is responsible for setting any balls that are dug when his team uses a three-hitter attack. The quick reactions and speed of the setter usually make him too valuable a digger to be assigned the area behind the block. In fact, some coaches place a big, slow spiker behind the block on defense to keep him out of the way. If this player is expected to set when the team switches from defense to offense, much individual coaching attention via the way of special drills is needed.

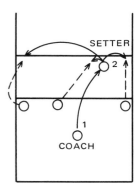

5

The Spike

The *spike* is an act of jumping in the air and hitting a set ball from above the level of the net into the opponents' court. It is an offensive play that usually drives the ball into the opponents' court with great force. Spiking requires a coordinated approach, jump and armswing at the moving ball.

Fig. 5.1 Teaching the Spike *When instructing children, it is necessary to lower the net to a point where the average child can touch the top of the tape with outstretched fingers while standing in the court. These seventh-grade girls are playing with a 6-ft. 6-in. net.* (Gary Adams)

a

b

Fig. 5.2   On-Hand and Off-Hand Spiking Positions   *From their on-hand side, spikers can usually watch the blockers without taking their eyes off the set. On the off-hand side, the set must travel across the spiker's body in front of the attacking arm or the spiker will not be able to observe the block closely.* (Dr. Leonard Stallcup)

The *on-hand* side of the court is that side on which the spiker would contact the ball with his predominant hand before it would cross in front of
his body. For example, the left front corner would be the on-hand side for
a right-handed spiker, as the ball would be contacted in front of the right
shoulder (Fig. 5.2a). If the ball is set to the right front corner, it travels across
the body to the right side before the spiker contacts the ball. This is more
difficult to perform and is known as the *off-hand* spike (Fig. 5.2b).

For the left-handed spiker, the on-hand and off-hand sides of the court
are reversed—*off-hand* is the left front, *on-hand* is the right front.

The preliminary position for the left front spiker is 8 to 12 ft. from the
net, near the left side line.

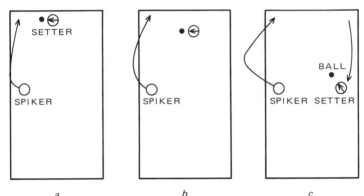

a   *b*   *c*

Fig. 5.3 Adjusting the Approach to the Pass   *The spiker must
anticipate where the pass will be directed and who will set the ball
while beginning the approach for the spike.*

Fig. 5.3 shows the following sequence. When the ball is passed close to
the net on his side of the court, the spiker must take a quick straight approach in order to receive a set that will travel a short distance (*a*). When
approaching during a good pass, most spikers prefer to swing slightly
outside the boundary line and approach the set at a slight angle so that they
can keep the ball and blockers in view at the same time (*b*). When a poor
pass is directed deep in the court, the primary setter usually cannot reach
the ball and a backcourt player becomes the setter. In this situation the
spiker should take a wide approach so that he can keep the player setting
the ball in full view as he moves toward the net (*c*).

The preliminary position for approaching the off-hand spike is the same
as for the on-hand, but from the opposite side of the court. If the setter
does not push the ball out to the side line, the hitter should move toward
the center of the court to allow the ball to cross his body until it is in front
of the attacking arm.

After the spiker reaches his preliminary position, he normally takes three
or four steps during his *approach for the spike*. He generally takes the last
step with his left leg if he is right-handed. The important point is that the
last step should be taken with the stronger leg regardless of the takeoff that
is used.

Fig. 5.4 Normal Approach for the Spike   *The player covers a distance of 10-12 ft. in three or four steps. He gradually increases the size and speed of his approach as he nears the takeoff point.* (Ealing Corp.)

The women on the prominent Japanese National Teams have been taught to take off by hopping on their power foot to land simultaneously with both heels parallel; next, they shift their weight to the balls of the feet and bend their legs, then forceably contract their legs, thereby forcing the spiker to leave the floor. The *hop takeoff* approach is used very infrequently by men and women participating in open and collegiate competition in the United States.

In the *step-close takeoff*, the spiker takes a long last step by jumping forward, contacting the floor first with the heel of one foot and then with the heel of the other foot; the weight then rolls from both heels to the toes as he takes off. When using this method, there is a tendency to broad jump when the spiker accelerates too quickly during the approach, or when he leans too far forward with the upper part of his body while preparing to jump.

The forward momentum which causes the spiker to broad jump can be overcome by keeping the upper part of the body at a right angle to the floor as the last step is taken. Spikers who prefer to use a rapid approach must jump slightly backward to transfer their forward momentum into a straight vertical jump.

The step-close takeoff approach is used almost exclusively by men and women participating in open and collegiate volleyball in the United States.

Fig. 5.5 Hop Takeoff *This approach is used almost exclusively by the women on the Japanese National Team. It allows them the greater body control that is needed for their quick, deceptive offense.*

Fig. 5.6 Step-Close Takeoff *It is important to contact the floor with the heels of both feet during the last steps so that the forward momentum of the body can be transferred into a vertical, rather than a broad jump.*

a

b

c

Fig. 5.7 Cocking the Spiking Hand Behind the Head   *The hand is held open or slightly cupped.* a *shows the front view;* b, *the back;* c, *the side.* (Los Angeles City Unified School District, *a*; Dr. Leonard Stallcup, *b*; Bud Fields, *c*)

In both the hop and step-close takeoff, arms are extended backward to approximately shoulder height, and swing down and forward in an arc as the heels hit the floor during the last step. By the time the weight shifts to the toes, the arms should be swinging forward and up above the shoulders as the player's legs and ankles forceably contract, moving the player into the air. As the player's hands reach head height, his back begins to arch and his legs bend backward at the knee. His left arm continues to rise until it reaches three-quarters to full extension above the shoulder. The right moves laterally above and behind the shoulder, and the hand is cocked behind the head. The body twists in the direction of the attacking arm and the left shoulder turns towards the net. The left arm drops quickly as the right arm uncoils toward the ball, with the elbow leading the way. The striking shoulder and upper body torque toward the ball as the body snaps forward from the waist. At contact the attacking arm is extended and the hand, either cupped or flat and stiff, is held open. As the wrist snaps forward, the heel and palm of the hand simultaneously contact the ball, followed by the fingers.

The ball should be hit above and in front of the attacking shoulder, slightly after the apex of the jump. After contact, the striking arm continues down and across the body. As the feet touch the floor, legs bend to absorb the impact.

Occasionally, a player may approach a high pass or set and take off on the leg opposite his attacking arm to spike the ball. *One-leg* takeoff does not allow the spiker the desired balance and control; it is used only to surprise

Fig. 5.8 Body Torque *Ernie Suwara twists the upper part of his body to deliver maximum power to his spike. In 1964, many experts considered Ernie to be the most powerful spiker to ever represent the USA.* (Dr. Leonard Stallcup)

a   *b*   *c*

Fig. 5.9 Contacting the Ball Above and In Front Of the Attacking Shoulder *When the spiker attempts to deceive the blockers, the ball is directed by turning the wrist in the direction of the intended flight.*

the block on the second touch of the ball or if the spiker does not have time to take a 2-ft. takeoff. The player who takes a 2-ft. takeoff to set or spike a pass can make his decision while in the air. The player who takes a 1-ft. takeoff has decided to spike before having left the floor.

The *trajectory* of a spiked ball must arc, as it is contacted further away from the net. On deeper sets the ball must be hit in an arc to land in the

Fig. 5.10 Hitting over the Block *This is accomplished with a maximum jump and fully extended spiking arm. Larry Rundle demonstrates perfect spiking form.* (Ealing Corp.)

a   *b*

Fig. 5.11 Arm and Hand Position During the Spike *This varies according to the distance the ball is set from the net. When spiking deep sets (a), the ball should be contacted over the attacking shoulder. When spiking a close set (b), the ball can be contacted up to 2 ft. in front of the attacking shoulder by spikers with a superior jump and reach.* (Ealing Corp.)

opponents' court. Effective spikers can hit the ball with full power at distances of 20 to 30 ft. from the net, and impart enough topspin to drive the ball into the opponents' court. To accomplish this, one hits the ball directly above or behind the attacking shoulder and makes contact below the ball's midline with the heel of his hand; he wraps his palm and fingers up and over the ball, producing maximum topspin with a vigorous wrist snap.

The height of the spiker's jump loses some if its significance when he can no longer hit the ball at an angle but must rely on maximum topspin to put the ball away. A deep set could be contacted below the level of the net and still be hit into the opponents' court with full power if the ball had enough topspin.

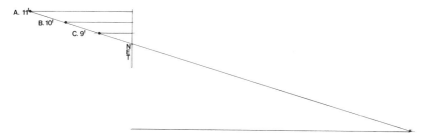

Fig. 5.12 Maximum Distances for Direct Angle Spikes A, *3 ft. above net at 10 ft. back;* B, *2 ft. above net at 7 ft. back;* C, *1 ft. above net at 3 ft. back.*

Fig. 5.12 illustrates the maximum depths to which spikers can hit the ball without imparting topspin, which causes the ball to drop or travel in an arc. For example, if a man was spiking the ball 10 ft. from the regulation 8-ft. net, he would have to contact the ball 3 ft. above the net to hit a direct angle spike into his opponents' court. In competition, these distances are shorter since balls that are spiked slightly above the top of the net can easily be blocked for a point.

The force of a spiked ball can be increased by arching the back and bending the knees at more than a 90-degree angle. The stomach and hip flexors then contract vigorously to snap the upper trunk and legs forward from the waist.

Spikers who contact the ball primarily with the heel of the hand will hit the ball with greater power than spikers who use the palm of the hand for most of the contact. Initial contact with the heel of the hand was popular until the blocking rules were changed in 1968. As soon as blockers were allowed to reach across the net, spiking tactics changed to emphasize placement and deception at the expense of power; therefore, most spikers favor contacting the ball higher on the hand.

An advantage of 2–3 in. in height may be gained by using the palm of the hand. Most players now favor contacting the ball higher on the hand for additional control as well as for extra height.

Experienced hitters with good peripheral vision can see *the hands of the*

a	*b*

Fig. 5.13 Power Spiking *Normal back arch and knee flexion are demonstrated (a). Additional knee and back flexion (b) add power to the spike but take away valuable inches from the spiker's vertical jump. This technique is used by many players on the Russian men's team.*

a	*b*

Fig. 5.14 Body Snap *This increases the power of the spike when the stomach and hip flexors vigorously contract during contact. All American left-handers Al Scates and Mary Jo Peppler demonstrate this technique.* (Bud Fields, *a*; Dr. Leonard Stallcup, *b*)

a	b

Fig. 5.15 Initial Contact with the Heel of the Hand *Bill Olsson (a) and Al Scates (b) demonstrate.* (Bud Fields)

a	b

Fig. 5.16 Initial Contact with the Palm of the Hand *This approach allows the spiker greater control at the expense of a slight reduction of power. It is the style used almost exclusively by better collegiate spikers.* (Bud Fields)

a   b

Fig. 5.17 Placing the Spike *Capable spikers can use the same approach and armswing to place the spike anywhere on the court by a last-moment turn of the wrist. Outward wrist rotation sends a spike cross court (a). Inward wrist rotation sends a spike down the line (b). (Ealing Corp.)*

Fig. 5.18 Cross Court Spike *Horace "Smitty" Duke, All World Volleyball player, gives every indication of a straight-ahead spike. He approaches the set with his shoulders parallel to the net and eludes the blockers with a perfect cross court turn of the wrist. (Bud Fields)*

defenders forming the block while leaping high in the air to spike the ball. Regardless of their approach to the set, they are capable of spiking the ball cross court or down the line by rotating their wrist and forearm inward or outward.

This ability to see the block generally takes two to three years of varsity competition, but it can be developed sooner by instructing blockers to move their hands either to the left or right just prior to the spiker's contact with the ball. The spiker will become aware of the blockers and learn to direct his spikes with greater accuracy.

A coach standing behind the spiker can easily signal the blockers to pull their hands left or right or to leave a hole in the middle of the block. If the spiker can successfully direct the ball through a hole in the block, it will seldom be fielded or "dug," since defensive alignments are built around the premise that the front row defenders will present a solid wall of hands to the spiker.

Spikers should learn to use the blocker's hands to their advantage, particularly on the balls set close to the net. Spikers who have the ability to see the blocker's hands can hit or "wipe" the ball off the block into the

Fig. 5.19 Line Spike   *High-flying Olympian Keith Erickson puts the ball by blockers Rudy Suwara and Jim Calonico.* (Bud Fields)

out-of-bounds area where it cannot be fielded. If the end blocker is small and cannot reach over the net with his outside hand to turn the ball into the court, the spiker should hit the ball hard so that it ricochets off his outside hand. This is an advanced technique and should be taught to experienced players only. Beginners tend to miss the hands and hit the ball out of bounds.

If the end blocker reaches over the net with his outside hand, the spiker should slow his armswing to confuse the blocker's timing and use his finger-

a

Fig. 5.20 Spiking Between the Blockers *The end blocker (a) has made the common mistake of moving past the 2-in. vertical tape marker that is fastened over the entire width of each side of the net. When the end blocker chases a wide set past the marker, the middle blocker has difficulty moving fast enough to close the hole (b). An alert spiker will place the ball through the opening. (Ealing Corp.)*

b

Fig. 5.21 Hitting the Ball off the End Blocker's Hand *Using this technique and hitting the ball into the out-of-bounds area almost always results in a point or side out.* (Bob Van Wagner)

Fig. 5.22 Lateral Wipe-Off Shot *Slowing the armswing and contacting the ball in a lateral motion, and then hitting the blocker's outside hand as he is descending usually prevents the blocker from maintaining the necessary height to keep his hand between the ball and side line. (Ealing Corp.)*

tips to impart "english," or lateral spin on the ball so that it is wiped off the blocker's hands into the out-of-bounds area. This is accomplished by moving the forearm and hand toward the side line at the last possible moment. This technique should be taught only to experienced spikers, who have the ability to watch the set and block at the same time.

When the spiker is trapped by a close set against tall, aggressive blockers, an effective shot is to hit the ball up, off the middle blocker's fingertips. In both the lateral and vertical wipe-off shots, the spiker runs the risk of the referee missing the blocker's touch of the ball and awarding his opponent a point or side out if the ball lands out of bounds. For this reason, a spiker must attempt to hit a good "piece" of the block, particularly if he is on the opposite side of the referee's stand.

a   *b*

Fig. 5.23 Vertical Wipe-Off Shot *This tactic is designed to keep the ball in play and does not usually score a point or side out unless the gym has a low ceiling.* (Ealing Corp.)

The vertical wipe-off shot is used to prevent the blocker from stuffing a close set back into the spiker's court.

The *round house spike* is a valuable weapon in the spiker's attack. It is used most effectively on a good set to confuse the opponents' block. In competition, it is usually seen when the spiker has run in front of the set or when the spiker is unable to get in position for a normal spike. Few men in this country have mastered the correct technique, and it is rarely attempted by women since the arm action requires more time off the floor than their jumping height normally allows.

The spiker takes a normal approach and jumps with his left arm extending in the usual manner. When his right arm reaches head height, it is rotated downward and backward in a windmill motion while extending.

Upon contact, the arm is fully extended over the shoulder. The ball is hit with the heel, palm and fingers tightly cupped. Since the arm action takes longer than the usual technique, the spiker always contacts the ball after he has reached the height of his jump. Opposing players are usually confused by this maneuver and are not in the optimum blocking position when the ball is hit.

THE DINK

The dink is a soft spike that is used to catch the defense off-guard. It is used most effectively on a good set when the defense is expecting a hard-driven spike. The attacker should cock his spiking arm in the normal manner and swing at a reduced speed to contact the ball with his fingertips.

Fig. 5.24 Arm Action   *Arm action of the one-hand dink closely resembles the spike. Most players make the mistake of "telegraphing" their intentions to the defense by straightening their arm too soon. Toshi Toyoda demonstrates the spiking action he uses when delivering the dink shot.* (Dr. Leonard Stallcup)

Contact is usually attempted as high above the net as possible so that the ball can be tipped over the block. All spikers should master the technique of *dinking over the middle blocker*. It keeps the defense "honest" and prevents it from always being in position to dig hard-driven spikes. The spiker who is skilled in varying his attack will be most effective. Shorter attackers may attempt to dink the ball into a tall blocker's forearms in the hope that the ball will roll down the opponent's body on the opposition's side of the net. When the low dink is attempted against a low block, the ball is usually stuffed to the floor.

Fig. 5.25 Contact *Contact should be made with the fingertips. The wrist should be held stiff.* (Dr. Leonard Stallcup)

a

b

Fig. 5.26 Dinking over the Middle Blocker *This is an effective way to score on the middle back defense. The wrist should be stiff, and contact should be made with the fingertips (a). Rudy Suwara dinks high above the blockers and follows through (b).*

Fig. 5.27 Alternate Tactic *Occasionally, an experienced attacker will dink the ball into the forearms of a tall blocker. The ball will ricochet to the floor on the opponents' side of the court if the blocker's arms are not over the net.* (Dr. Leonard Stallcup)

Fig. 5.28 Dinking Against a Three-Man Block *This is always good strategy because the three remaining backcourt players will find it extremely difficult to cover the entire court.* (Bud Fields)

Fig. 5.29 Two-Handed Dink Shot
Larry Rundle attempts to draw a touch of the blockers' fingers as he releases the ball toward his opponents' back line. (Dr. Leonard Stallcup)

Fig. 5.30 Keeping the Ball in Play *An overhand lob into the block usually results in the ball rebounding softly back into the attackers' court, allowing the offense to recover the ball and giving them another chance to put the ball away.* (Bud Fields)

Fig. 5.31 Punching the Ball *Punching the ball over the net with a closed fist is recommended only when the ball drops below the level of the net prior to contact.* (Los Angeles City Unified School District)

When three blockers are defending against the attacker, there is a lot of court left open for a well-placed dink shot.

The *two-handed dink shot* is usually used to place the ball deep in the opponents' court or to rebound the ball off the blockers' hands to keep the ball in play.

When a close set drops below the level of the net, it can be punched over with the knuckles. This type of dink is a last resort in the regulation six-man game, used merely to keep the ball in play. In two-man volleyball the open-hand dink is often interpreted as a throw. Thus, the closed-fist technique is common in doubles volleyball.

OFF-SPEED SPIKE

The off-speed spike is effective only when the defense is braced for a hard kill. If the spiker is off-balance or does not use a normal approach, the defense will expect the spiker to hit the ball with less force. The speed of the striking arm is reduced just prior to contact to confuse the defense. If the spiker uses his normal approach and a slower armswing, the blockers will lose their timing and the backcourt defenders will find the ball losing momentum and landing in front of them. The off-speed spike is most effective when used infrequently and when directed toward a definite weakness in the defense—whether it be an individual or open area of the court.

Fig. 5.32 Off-Speed Spike *With a turn of his wrist, player No. 8 directs a half-speed spike through a hole in the block.* (Dr. Leonard Stallcup)

SPIKING THE LOW VERTICAL SET

The most exciting offensive play in volleyball utilizes split-second timing between spiker and setter; it is a well-executed spike of a low vertical set.

The low vertical set, or one-set, is extremely important to the success of the three-hitter offense.

Spiking the low vertical set was popularized among athletes and spectators in the United States by the touring Japanese National Men's and Women's teams shortly after the 1964 Olympic Games. It was perfected by the Japanese to make the small spiker effective and to create one-on-one blocking situations for their strong spikers.

The spiker approaches to within a few feet of the setter as he moves into position to receive the pass. If he intends to spike the ball as soon as it rises above the net, he gathers to jump and is in the air before the setter touches the ball. His spiking arm is cocked with little body torque or shoulder rotation, ready and waiting for the setter to deliver the ball in front of his attacking arm. He should be at the apex of his jump just as the ball is clearing the tape at the top of the net. He contacts the set a few inches after it rises above the net.

There is little opportunity for the spiker to consciously direct his spike using this technique. The emphasis is on quickly hitting the ball to the floor on a sharp downward flight—not on power. If the ball is contacted before

| a | b |

Fig. 5.33 Spiking a Low Vertical Set *George Conkey delivers the low vertical, or* one-set, to spiker Mike Allio.

it crosses his attacking shoulder, it is usually hit to his right (Fig. 5.33a). If the set is contacted in front of or past his attacking shoulder, it is normally hit straight ahead or to the left *(Fig. 5.33b)*. Better spikers will learn to direct the ball to any area of the court while using several different approach patterns.

When a spiker has mastered the technique of hitting the low vertical set just as it leaves the setter's fingertips, the opposing blocker must jump with the attacker to block successfully. Defending against the low vertical set requires the middle blocker to jump with the middle attacker before the ball is set. The play was developed to force the middle blocker to commit himself in this manner so that the other two spikers would have the opportunity to receive a normal set against one blocker. The proficient setter must watch the middle blocker, the ball and the approaching spiker while deciding to deliver the ball.

In a three-hitter attack, this places the other two spikers in a one-on-one situation with the end blockers. In *Fig. 5.37* the setter has elected to deliver a high wide set to the outside spiker (No. 11) before the middle blocker can recover to form a two-man block. Since the middle blocker is usually the most proficient, this technique takes on added significance when a weak spiker is able to take the opposition's best blocker out of the play with a feigned attack.

When the middle attacker constantly forces the middle blocker to jump with him, the best percentage play is usually a high wide set to the on-hand spiker. The middle blocker cannot recover fast enough to join the end

Fig. 5.34 Defending Against the Low Vertical Set *Toshi Toyoda (No. 1) prepares to deliver a set over his head to the off-hand spiker (not shown). Player No. 14 takes the middle blocker out of the play.*

Fig. 5.35 Setting the On-Hand Spiker *Player No. 11 approaches from the on-hand side while No. 9 holds the middle blocker. Toshi Toyoda (No. 1) sets.*

Fig. 5.36 A Maximum Jump by the Middle Attacker   *A jump by the middle attacker is necessary because he never knows if the setter will deliver the ball to him or another spiker. Toshi Toyoda leaps high above the net as teammate No. 1 delivers a set over Toshi's head to the on-hand spiker (not shown).* (Dr. Leonard Stallcup)

blocker if he has left the floor, and the on-hand spiker has the opportunity to attack from his power side against one blocker.

When a spiker becomes proficient at hitting low sets, the setter may choose to deliver the ball to him even though one defender will always block against him. In this case the spiker may elect to jump after the ball is released and hit a slightly higher set, generally called a two-set.

The spiker contacts the two-set at the top of its flight; consequently, he will have enough time to use normal armswing and body torque to spike the ball in any direction. The set should be low enough to prevent a two-man block and high enough to allow the spiker to place the ball accurately. When a valuable spiker is attacking from the middle, it is usually good strategy to use a two-set.

Spikers with quick reflexes and good coordination will be able to hit the ball inches out of the setter's hands when the setter jumps to receive a pass that is high and close to the net.

Fig. 5.37 Approach for a Two-Set   *Tom Madison is preparing to jump for a two-set slightly after Toshi Toyoda releases the ball.*

In Fig. 5.39 the setter has jumped, extended his arms and flicked the set with his fingertips to compensate for the spiker's early approach. If the spiker was late, he would lower his arms before contacting the ball to give the spiker time to arrive at the contact point.

The low vertical set, or one-set, is almost always attempted from the on-hand side so that the setter does not have to push the ball across the attacker's body in front of his attacking arm.

The most difficult offensive play in volleyball is a *back one-set to an off-hand spiker*. This play is difficult because the setter can only watch the ball and the opposing blocker. The spiker's timing must be perfect since the setter will only hear his footsteps and can rarely compensate for a poor approach. Since this play is rarely attempted, it usually leaves the blocker standing on the floor when executed correctly.

Fig. 5.38 Spiking the Two-Set *Kirk Kilgour has just received the set from his teammate. The team passed the ball to its left so that Kilgour could attack from the middle position on his on-hand side.* (Bob Van Wagner)

Fig. 5.39 Spiking a Jump One-Set
This play is used when the first pass is delivered too close to the net. Ernie Suwara leaps high above the net to deliver a one-set to Larry Rundle, who will hit the ball inches out of Ernie's fingertips.

Fig. 5.40 Back One-Set to the Off-Hand Spiker *Ernie Suwara sets to Larry Rundle.*

SPIKING A SHOOT SET

The shoot set is delivered low and fast to create one-on-one blocking situations. It is usually placed a few feet from the side line and contacted at a height of 1–2 ft. above the net, depending on the preference and vertical jump of the spiker. The set is extremely difficult for the middle blocker to cover when the ball travels a distance of 10 ft. or more from setter to spiker. This is the best method of creating a one-on-one spiking situation in the two-hitter attack. The spiker should start his approach closer to the net and slightly outside the side line. Normal takeoff and spiking technique should be used.

In a three-hitter attack a shoot set is called a "three" when utilized by the middle spiker to split the end and middle blockers. It is a very quick, low trajectory set that requires the same split-second timing as the low vertical set.

Ideally, the ball is passed to the setter at a point 2 ft. from the net and about 10 ft. from the right side line. The spiker quickly moves to a point about 10 ft. from the left side line between the end and middle blockers. The spiker should time his approach so that he jumps as the ball is being released from the setter.

In Fig. 5.41, the middle blocker is late and cannot close in fast enough to touch the ball. After setting, Toshi Toyoda moves forward to back up the spiker.

Fig. 5.41 Middle Spiker Attacking a Three-Set *Tom Madison alertly dinks the ball over the end blocker who has moved from the side line but has not had time to leave the floor.* (Bob Van Wagner)

SPIKING DRILLS

Most of the following drills can also be used to improve dinks, off-speed shots and round house spikes. To increase the difficulty, add blockers or an entire defensive alignment.

Spikers line up near the left side line, about 12 ft. from the net. Work on long and short line spikes. Repeat the drill from the right side line.

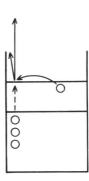

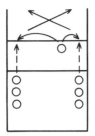

Use a straight approach and spike the ball cross court. Place a towel on the floor for the spiker to hit.

Using an angle approach from the on-hand side, spike the ball down the side line.

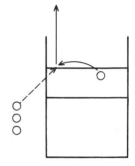

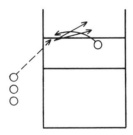

Using an angle approach from the on-hand side, spike the ball cross court.

Using two lines of spikers and one setter, set either side. The spiker should not rotate until he hits.

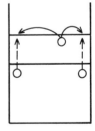

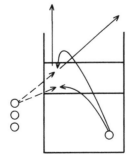

Spike a backcourt set cross court and down the line. Vary height and placement of the set.

Spikers hit a low vertical set. The setter stations himself 10 ft. from the right side line, a foot from the net.

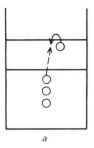

a

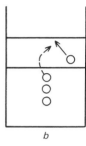

b

The coach passes the ball to the setter at various locations inside the 10-ft. line. The spiker must adjust his approach to the pass to get in a favorable position to hit a low quick set.

Spikers hit a shoot set from the left side.

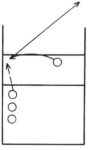

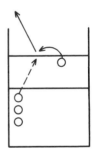

End spikers hit a shoot set 10 ft. from the left side line.

Middle spikers hit a shoot set 10 ft. from the left side line.

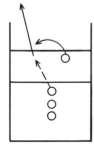

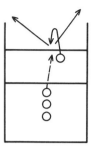

Middle spikers hit a front two-set.

Off-hand spikers hit a back two-set.

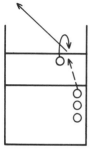

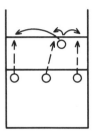

Three spikers work with one setter.

Spikers practice hitting the ball over the blocker's hands. Blockers can stand on a bench to regulate their height.

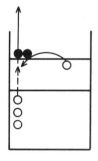

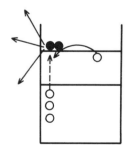

Spikers practice hitting the ball off the end blocker's hand into the out-of-bounds area.

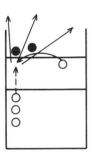

As the set is in the air, the blockers leave a vulnerable spot in the block. The spiker must hit through the hole.

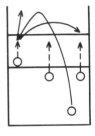

A backcourt player passes the ball to the front row setter, who spikes or jump sets to his teammate.

Recover a blocked spike and set the ball to a front row player. Pass the ball to the setter if he does not field the blocked spike.

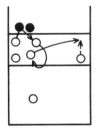

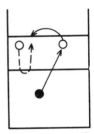

The player simulates a block and, as he is returning to the floor, the coach throws the ball to a teammate who sets him.

The coach throws balls over the net for players in blocking positions to hit sharply downward or set.

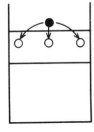

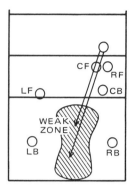

The end spiker attacks weak areas of the man in defense by using dinks, off-speed shots and spikes.

The middle spiker attacks weak areas of the man in defense by dinking and using off-speed shots to the front corners and hitting the ball over or off the blocker's fingertips to the deep corners.

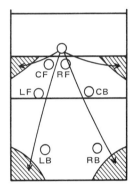

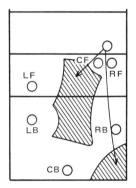

The end spiker attacks weak areas of the man back defense by dinking and hitting off-speed shots into the center of the court and driving long spikes over or off the fingertips of the end blockers.

The middle spiker attacks weak areas of the man back defense by dinking and using off-speed shots to the front corners and deep spikes to the back corners.

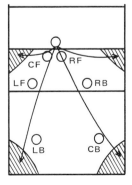

The end spiker attacks weak areas of the off-blocker defense by hitting a sharp angle inside the middle blocker or dinking and hitting off-speed spikes down the line.

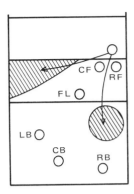

6

The Block

The *block* is a defensive play by one or more players who attempt to intercept the ball near the net. Blocking is permitted by any or all of the players in the front line. Blockers are allowed to reach as far over the net as possible as long as they do not touch the ball before the offense has attacked. The most common type of block is a two-man block.

When one or more players participate in the block and make only one attempt to block the ball, they may make successive contacts of the ball and it only counts as one hit. A player participating in the block may participate in the next play and it counts as the second of three hits allowed to the team.

The most effective way to demoralize a team is by not allowing the star spiker to hit the ball over the net. Good spikers find it increasingly difficult to put the ball away, as the opposition realizes the importance of aligning its best blockers against them. Often an aggressive block will score over 50 percent of a team's points—either indirectly (intimidates the opponents to use poor percentage shots to avoid the block) or directly (blocks ball to the floor). Blocking specialists can substitute across the front row up to three times in one game, and can often force opposing setters to deliver the ball 5–6 ft. back from the net to protect their spikers.

INDIVIDUAL BLOCKING TECHNIQUE

Blocking technique will vary according to the reach and vertical jump of the blocker.

a

b

c

d

e

f

Fig. 6.1 The Block   *The block is a defensive play in which any or all front court players place one or two hands above their head while in a position close to the net. a and* b *show one blocker;* c *and* d, *two blockers;* e *and* f, *three blockers.* (Bud Fields; Dr. Leonard Stallcup)

Shorter players and blockers with average armswing may need to take a short run of two or three steps while using a full armswing to increase the height of their jump. This approach should be used only if the blocker cannot achieve the necessary height by using one step. As the blocker moves further away from the net, he increases the risk of netting or crossing the center line while landing. Taller players or good jumpers should rarely move more than a step away from the net for their approach.

Fig. 6.2 Blocking for Points *Blocking for points can contribute up to 50 percent of a team's total score.*

Blockers should experiment with the angle of the squat, or gather, used to prepare for the jump in order to determine what degree of leg flexion gives them the greatest vertical jumping height. Small players may utilize a full squat whereas taller blockers may be more effective using a one-third to half-squat.

Exceptional jumpers may use a standing takeoff without a full armswing. By eliminating excessive body movements, the blocker is able to wait for the spiker to commit himself and use better body control to counter his opponent's attack.

The blocker must achieve the necessary vertical jump to stop the attack by starting as close to the net as his height and jumping ability will allow.

A simple test to measure a player's jumping reach is administered by chalking the middle fingertips of both hands and measuring the lowest touch mark on a wall after a vertical jump. If a Sargent Jump Board is available, set the zero line at net height for quicker evaluation. This jump test can aid in the determination of the blocking style that is to be used by your blockers. After a thorough warm-up, the player should be tested on the following jumping techniques:

- A standing jump with hands held at shoulder height
- A standing jump with full armswing
- A one-step approach with full armswing
- A longer approach if none of the foregoing techniques have yielded an adequate height

a   b   c

Fig. 6.3 Sargent Jump Test   *The player stands flat-footed, feet together, toes and chest against the wall. He places his fingertips underneath the board and pushes it up until his arms are fully extended(a). Then he turns sideways to the wall and squats to the desired level (b). He jumps and reaches, one hand touching as far up the board as possible (c). The score is the difference between the reach while standing and jumping.*

The player should be allowed to flex his knees at the angle of his choice for the first three jumps in every test. Normally, players will not squat low enough to produce maximum jumping height until instructed to do so. Most volleyball players have played basketball since elementary school and consequently have not been trained to utilize a low squat for added height. Rebounding does not give a player the necessary time to prepare for the maximum jump that is utilized to block the spike of a high, wide set. The coach can point this out rather dramatically after the first person tested increases his vertical jump by squatting lower to bring the stronger quadriceps and *gluteus maximus* muscles into play to aid the muscles of the calf.

Unless fatigue becomes a factor, jumping height will increase as the player uses an armswing and approach. Since better control is achieved without

a

b

c

Fig. 6.4 Blocking a Spiker with Normal Armswing *The blockers must jump shortly after the spiker leaves the floor. When the ball is set further away from the net, the blockers must hesitate before jumping to give the spike an additional split second to travel the added distance to the net.* (Ealing Corp.)

a

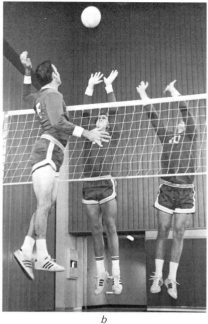

b

c

Fig. 6.5   Blocking a Spiker with Late Armswing
This blocking technique should be used only if
the scouting report indicates that the spiker is
habitually late in contacting the ball. (Ealing Corp.)

a full armswing and standing takeoff, the point of this test is to determine if an approach and armswing are necessary. The average end blocker will find it necessary to use a one-step approach when opposing tall spikers, and a standing approach to block smaller players and teams that use quick, low sets.

Some end blockers may have to use an approach on every block, while outstanding jumpers and taller players may be able to use a standing takeoff with little or no armswing. Smaller players will usually jump higher using a two-thirds to full squat, whereas tall blockers will generally be more efficient using a half-squat or less.

Most of the time the blocker will jump shortly after the spiker has left the floor.

Since spikers use a longer approach, they are able to jump higher and remain in the air longer than blockers. If the blockers jump with the spiker on a normal set, they will be too low when the spiker contacts the ball. Blockers must wait even longer when the ball is set deep in their opponents' court. Some spikers create the illusion of "hanging" in the air by spiking the ball on the way down.

Blockers must constantly remind themselves to hesitate when facing an opponent who spikes the ball on the way down and use a late armswing.

Fig. 6.5 shows how to block a spiker with late armswing. Blockers must discipline themselves to stay on the floor until the spiker nears the apex of his jump. Blockers should time their movement so that they are at the height of their jump as the late spiker is contacting the ball on his return

a   *b*

Fig. 6.6 Late Takeoff by Short Middle Blockers   *This technique allows short middle blockers to reach the same height as their taller teammates when the spike approaches the net. (Bob Van Wagner, a; Dr. Leonard Stallcup, b)*

Fig. 6.7 **Defending Against a Quick Middle Set** *All American spiker Ed Becker is in the air to spike a set from All American Toshi Toyoda against a well-positioned blocker.*

to the floor. Better spikers are capable of defeating this blocking tactic by switching to a quick armswing and hitting over the blocker's hands.

A short blocker must have perfect timing to block the middle position because his hands cannot remain above the net as long as his taller teammates. A taller man can jump too soon and still block the spike, but the short blocker is up and down relatively fast.

Short blockers should normally jump after their taller teammates, particularly when facing a very tall spiker. The blocker who has his toes on the floor in Fig. 6.6a is 5 ft. 11 in.; his opponent spiker, who uses a late armswing, is 6 ft. 7 in. The late jumping blocker will leave the floor just prior to the hit and attempt to contact the spike at the height of his jump.

When the setter delivers a quick, low set to a spiker who is capable of hitting the ball inches out of the setter's hand, the blocker must jump with the spiker (Fig. 6.7). In this situation, jumping ability is not as important as agility.

After takeoff, there are variations in the arm motion. As the player jumps, his arms are raised from below the waist, passed over his chest and face and fully extended when the blocker is at the fullest height of his jump. Some players will be able to extend their forearms from 18–24 in. over the net, while the great majority of blockers will only be able to extend their forearms to the top of the net and reach over with their wrists and hands.

Fig. 6.8 Spiking Through the Block *A slight closing of the blocker's arms and hands would have blocked the spike.* (Bob Van Wagner)

Tall blockers with superior jump can utilize a different technique. They should crouch with their hands above shoulder level and extend their arms over the net as they jump. The advantage of this technique is added body control, which allows greater concentration on the intentions of the approaching spiker.

Regardless of the style that is used, the distance between the hands and portions of the arms above the net at the moment of contact normally should be less than the circumference of the ball.

The obvious results of leaving a wider space in the block are shown in Fig. 6.8. When the ball is set outside the court, the blocker may widen the space between his hands due to the angle of flight the ball must travel to legally pass the side line markers on the net.

As the blocker descends, his arms and hands draw away from the net and down the sides of his body. The shock of landing is absorbed by his toes, soles and heels of both feet and then his legs. If the ball does not rebound into the opponents' court, the blocker turns his head in the direction of the spike as he descends so that he will be ready for the next play.

ATTACK BLOCK

The attack block is an attempt to intercept the ball before it crosses the net. Blockers may reach across the net but may not contact the ball until their opponent has attempted to hit the ball across the net.

Fig. 6.9 Attack Block *The attack block has revolutionized the game by forcing setters to place the ball deep in their own court to prevent the blockers from rebounding the spike back into the attacking team's court.* (Bud Fields)

Fig. 6.10 Teaching the Attack Block *The seventh-grade girls (foreground) are playing doubles volleyball with a 6-ft. 6-in. net. The younger children (background) are using a lower net.* (Gary Adams)

Blockers should extend their arms above the net and move them downward from the shoulders, tilting their wrists forward while keeping their hands and fingers rigid.

Ideally, contact with the ball should be made with the heels of the hand just as the body is descending. In competition, spikes are also blocked with forearms, palms and fingers.

The capable blocker will always attack block when in good position and when the offense consists of fast, low sets. If the spiker receives a low set close to the net, the blocker should form a "roof" around the ball with his hands, leaving the spiker trapped.

SOFT BLOCK

Blockers should also master the technique of soft blocking. The soft block is usually recommended when the ball is set away from the net. It is called a soft block because a blocked ball rebounds back into the opponents'

Fig. 6.11 Soft Block *Blockers may keep their hands above the net longer and cover a greater area above the net. Deep spikes, which are usually not hit with as much force as a close spike, are easier to slow up or deflect to a teammate.* (Bud Fields)

court at a lesser angle and slower speed. The forearms are held parallel to the net, hands held either tilted back or parallel to the net.

Smaller blockers must use the soft block a majority of the time so that they can reach high above the net to prevent spikers from hitting the ball over their hands. There are many occasions that call for the blocker to attempt to slow up the spike and deflect the ball to a teammate. A blocker can cover a much greater area above the net by attempting to deflect a spike than he can by reaching over the net. In Fig. 6.12, blocker No. 1 has chosen to slow up a cross court spike.

When the middle blocker must swing his arms toward the end blocker to shut off the path of the oncoming spike, he will often find himself too far away from the net. To prevent the ball from striking his hands and falling between himself and the net, he should tilt his hands back to deflect the ball to a teammate (blocker on the right, Fig. 6.13).

Blockers should normally use the soft block to intercept deep spikes. Blockers must jump after the spiker when the spiker is hitting a ball that is not set close to the net. If blockers jump with the spiker, they will not have

Fig. 6.12 Attempting to Deflect the Spike *One blocker is trying to cover a large area of the net.* (Bob Van Wagner)

Fig. 6.13 Combination Blocks *The end blocker is making an attack block and the middle blocker is making a soft block. Although he is soft blocking, the blocker's hands (right) should be closer to the net.*

the necessary height to block effectively by the time the ball approaches the net. The soft block allows the blocker a greater margin of time to assess the direction and speed of a deep spike.

In Fig. 6.13, the middle blocker hopes to close the hole between the blockers; he must move his arms laterally and is sometimes prevented from reaching over the net (particularly if he is slightly late in arriving at the point of attack).

TWO-MAN BLOCK

In the preliminary position, the right blocker should start about 2 ft. from the side line, the left end blocker about 4 ft. from the other side line, with the middle blocker splitting the distance between them.

For right- or left-handed spikers, there are easier and more difficult spikes to perform, depending upon which side of the court the ball is set to. These are called "on-hand" and "off-hand" spikes. The on-hand ·side of the court is the side on which the spiker could contact the ball with his predominant hand before it could cross in front of his body. For example, the left front corner would be the on-hand side for a right-handed spiker, as the ball would not cross in front of his body before it was contacted in front of his right shoulder. Most right-handed spikers are capable of spiking the ball down the side line by rotating their forearms and wrists inward on the power

Fig. 6.14 Starting Distance *A blocker's starting distance from the net is determined by his height, vertical jump, reach and individual style. The small end blocker in the background is taking a 3-ft. approach to combat high-spiking Larry Rundle.* (Ealing Corp.)

Fig. 6.15 Turning the Spike In *This player reaches over the net with his outside hand between the boundary line and the ball to cut off the possibility of a "wipe-off" shot. Turning the spike in is a difficult skill to master and must constantly be stressed in practice.*

side. This is the reason why the right end blocker must start closer to the side line than his counterpart on the left side when the attackers are right-handed.

When blocking a spiker on his off-hand side, start about 4 ft. from the side line; when blocking an on-hand spiker, start about 2 ft. from the side line. If the spiker demonstrates a good line shot on his off-hand side, start closer to the side line.

The end blocker should always use the *slide step*, which is initiated by pointing the outside foot in the direction of movement and taking a long step sideways. The other foot slides toward the first, and the action is repeated without changing body position or crossing the legs. Shoulders remain parallel to the net throughout the slide step. After the ball leaves the setter, the blocker watches the attacking spiker and converges to the point at which the spiker must contact the ball.

The end blocker protects his side line by lowering his inside shoulder and by moving his outside hand along the top of the net toward the ball with a sweeping motion.

When the blocker contacts the ball, his outside hand should be between the ball and side line. This prevents the ball from being "wiped off" the blocker's hands into the out-of-bounds area where the backcourt men cannot reach it.

When a blocker senses that the spiker may deliberately hit the ball toward the out-of-bounds area in an attempt to contact his hand, he should quickly drop his hand below the level of the net to allow the spike to travel out of bounds.

The end blocker's primary responsibility is to position the block on wide sets.

The objective of the end blocker on a normal set is to align himself so that both he and the middle blocker will block the ball on their inside hands. If middle blockers are late, the backcourt will find themselves continually out of position in attempting to cover their teammates. When the ball is set to the center spiker, the outside blocker from whom the ball is set toward will join the middle blocker. This enables the defense to use a normal four-man digging pattern. Occasionally, all three front court players will be required to block a superior center spiker; however, if the ball gets by the block, there are only three diggers left to cover the entire court.

If a *three-man block* is used, the two end blockers turn the ball in with their outside hands, the other four hands reaching over and parallel to the net.

Center blockers should master the slide and the crossover steps.

The slide step is slightly slower and does not allow the blocker to jump as high as the crossover, but does have the advantage of allowing the blocker to arrive at the point of attack under full control. Tall blockers with good

Fig. 6.16 Hitting Off the End Blocker   *Larry Millikin, 1969 USVBA Player of the National Collegiate Tournament, drives a spike off Kirk Kilgour's (No. 13) outside hand.* (Dr. Leonard Stallcup)

a

b

Fig. 6.17 Tight Block   *When backcourt diggers do not have to concentrate on spikes coming through the block, they can position themselves to field spikes hit around the block and increase their effectiveness.* (Dr. Leonard Stallcup, a; Ealing Corp., b)

vertical jump and quick reactions should use the slide step most of the time.

The traditional approach is the *crossover step*, which is slightly faster than the slide step and allows the blocker to gain additional height on the jump. The first step is a crossover with the inside foot, which turns the body at a 90-degree angle to the net; the second step is long, and the third step puts the blocker in position for the normal 2-ft. takeoff used in the jump. At the completion of the second step, the legs should be flexed and arms extended backwards almost at shoulder level. The arms drive downward, pointing toward the floor as the player completes his third step, and then forward and up as the player forceably extends his legs to drive himself off the floor.

If the blocker arrives at the point of attack early, he can pivot to face the net during his second step so that his shoulders are parallel to the net as he completes his third step. He must lean back as his outside foot contacts

Fig. 6.18 Spiking Between the Blockers *No workable defense can cover a hole between the blockers. Backcourt players must rush to cover the blockers' error.* (Bob Van Wagner)

the floor in order to transfer his lateral momentum into a vertical jump. If the blocker is late, he will have to turn while in mid-air. Many blockers lack the necessary coordination to turn and block in mid-air. If they fail to learn this technique after reasonable practice and are not quick enough to use the slide step, they will not be able to block successfully in the middle position.

A mobile blocker using the crossover technique should easily be able to move 12 ft. in three steps. Since the volleyball court is 30 ft. wide, that is as far as he will normally have to travel to close in on the end blocker.

Another advantage of the crossover step is that it allows the blocker to use almost the same armswing and jump that he utilizes in spiking. This adds valuable inches to his vertical jump.

An alternate to the crossover is to pivot simultaneously toward the side line and drive off the inside foot while stepping in the direction of movement with the outside foot. Then the inside foot takes a long step and pivots so that the blocker's shoulders are parallel to the net as he completes his third step. If the blocker is late, he will have to turn toward the net while in mid-air. The pivot and drive method also utilizes the approach and armswing used during the spike and should easily cover a distance of 12 ft. if necessary.

Generally, a right-handed spiker will have a stronger left leg and vice versa. The spiker will almost invariably take the last step in his spiking approach with his strongest leg, which normally results in greater jumping height. If this principle were applied to blocking, the right-handed middle blocker would normally use the crossover step when moving to his right; he would use the pivot and drive step when moving to his left.

When blocking the middle position, women may have to use more than three steps to arrive at the point of attack. The first and last steps are the same, but additional steps may have to be added to cover the distance to the takeoff point.

BLOCKING STRATEGY

Normally, the most effective blocker switches to the center, the next strongest blocker to the power side, and the third blocker to the weak or off-hand side.

The middle position allows a mobile blocker to participate in almost all of the blocks against a two-hitter attacker, as well as in the majority of the blocks against a three-hitter attack. Since most teams set the spiker on his

Fig. 6.19 Forcing the Spiker to Hit Cross Court   *Blockers Tom Ryan and Dick Montgomery take away the line to enable digger in the background to be in an excellent position to dig Larry Rundle's spike. Rudy Suwara and Dan Patterson are backing up the spiker.* (Bob Van Wagner)

Fig. 6.20 Helping the End Blocker *Effective middle blockers with good jumping ability learn to reach over their small teammates when necessary.* (Bud Fields)

on-hand side significantly more than on his off-hand side, the next best blocker usually switches to his right. This generally leaves the remaining blocker to cover an off-hand spiker. Through the course of the season, many teams become predictable in their attack and try to set the ball to a particular spiker in a certain rotation. A simple attack chart kept on the opposition will tell the coach how to position his blockers in each rotation.

The coach should instruct his blockers to go after the ball or to protect a given area of the net. For example, the blockers may protect the line and force the spiker to hit cross court. The obvious advantage of this tactic is that the backcourt defenders can usually predict where the ball will be hit. The disadvantage is that the blocker becomes less aggressive and does not directly score as many points. A good middle blocker should never be

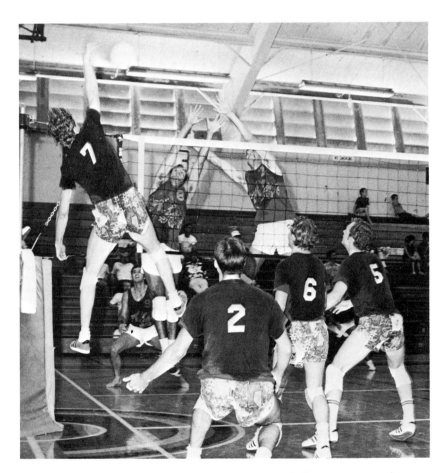

Fig. 6.21 Overlapping Block Coverage   *Experienced blockers can sometimes "read" the spiker's intentions to the degree that two blockers do the job of one (both cover the same area).* (Dr. Leonard Stallcup)

instructed to zone block when playing next to a small or inefficient blocker. Since opposing spikers will continually attempt to hit over the smaller blocker, the middle blocker must have the freedom to key on the ball.

When the blockers are instructed to go aggressively after the ball, the backcourt players must constantly adapt to the changing patterns of the block. Unless backcourt players are capable of reacting very quickly, they will not dig as many balls. An additional hazard is that blockers begin to overact to the ball to such an extent that they begin to interfere with each other. To prevent this from happening, the coach should instruct the players to concentrate on protecting a given area of the net rather than aggressively moving toward the ball.

A *false weakness* in the block is employed occasionally to stop better spikers who like to watch the block closely. An example is the blocker who positions himself well inside the line and, in effect, issues an invitation to the spiker to hit outside his position. When the spiker starts his armswing, the blocker quickly closes the unprotected area by moving his arms toward the line. The initial jump brings a blocker to his starting point; through lateral movement of his arms, an effective blocker can protect from 4–5 ft. of the net.

In Fig. 6.22, the blocker in effect issues an invitation to the spiker to hit to a certain area of the court. Then he attempts to block that area at the last

a

b

Fig. 6.22 Closing the Unprotected Zone   *Experienced blockers use this effective tactic against experienced spikers who watch the block before they contact the ball. Andy Banachowski demonstrates proper arm movement (a) in his initial position; in b, he shows lateral movement.*

split second. If the blocker does not alert his backcourt teammates as to his intention, they will take themselves out of the play by rushing to fill a hole that the blocker will close.

The same false weakness can be used to draw the spike to the middle or inside of the block. This blocking technique would be futile against beginning players, who simply jump and hit the ball as hard as possible, regardless of where the block has formed.

READING THE SPIKER

Spikers usually attempt to avoid the block by hitting the ball cross court or down the line. The better blockers will know whether the normal spiker plans to hit inside or outside the block. He can judge this by analyzing or "reading" the spiker's approach to the set, his body alignment and, most important, his armswing. All spikers give some indication of where they plan to hit the ball, although better spikers try to conceal their intentions until the last split second or when the blockers are in mid-air. This limits the blocker's lateral movement to about 2–3 ft. in any direction.

The following hints will help the blocker to "read" or analyze certain types of spikers and situations.

1. The spiker with a right angle or straight approach to the net is in a good position to hit a line shot.

2. An "on-hand" spiker can hit the line shot with greater accuracy and power than an "off-hand" spiker.

3. Short spikers usually have developed a good line shot.

4. When the ball is set close to the side line, it is easy for the spiker to hit the ball down the line.

5. Off-hand spikers who begin their approach off the court will usually have a weak line shot.

6. The spiker will almost always hit the ball cross court on a low, quick set.

7. Inexperienced and average spikers hit significantly more cross court angles than line shots from both the strong and weak sides.

8. As balls are set farther away from the net, the tendency to hit cross court is increased.

9. When blocking a taller player or a spiker with a slow or late armswing, the blocker should jump later than he normally does.

10. If the spiker runs under the ball, expect a high, flat spike or an off-speed shot.

11. A slow approach or lack of height on the· jump usually indicates an off-speed spike.

12. Tired or off-balance spikers tend to dink or hit off the blocker's hands.

13. Prior to the serve, signals are often exchanged between the spiker and

Fig. 6.23 Simultaneous Blocks *These are usually blown dead by the official. The ball must bounce off the blocker or blockers in a legal manner.*

the setter. Close observation of verbal or hand signals will often tell the blocker what type of play to expect.

14. A closer starting position prior to the spiker's approach indicates that there is a play.

15. If the set travels inside the spiker's attacking shoulder, he will probably hit the ball across his body.

16. Do not block an average spiker on a poor set.

17. Every opposing spiker has favorite shots. *Learn them.*

COMMON ERRORS

There are several common errors that players make while attempting to block.

- Touching the net
  Caused by jumping forward or laterally; blockers should jump straight up into the air.
  Caused by extending arms in front of the body during the jump instead of raising them vertically.
  Caused by reaching too far over the net; blockers must learn their safe range of attack blocking.
- Ball bounces down the front of the body on blockers' side of the net
  Caused by jumping too far from the net.
  Caused by slow arm and hand extension over the net.
  Leaving too large a space between hands and forearms.
- Constantly missing the spike
  Caused by dipping the head or closing the eyes; blockers should know why every ball went past his hands. If he does not, he should force himself to keep his eyes on the ball after the spiker attacks.
  Caused by watching the ball instead of the spiker. Primary attention

Fig. 6.24 Jumping Too Far from the Net *If the blocker touches the spike, the ball usually bounces down the front of the body on the blockers side of the net. This is a common error of beginning players.*

Fig. 6.25 Hitting Through the Blocker
This occurs if the blocker's hands are further apart than the width of the ball, or if the hands are held too loosely and the ball squirts through rather than rebounds into the spiker's court.
(Dr. Leonard Stallcup)

should be focused on the approaching spiker, as the ball will come into view as it nears the spiking arm.

Caused by blockers not moving close enough to each other and leaving a hole in the middle of the block. (see Fig. 6.18)

● The ball ricochets off the hands and goes out of bounds

Caused by presenting a flat surface of the outside hand instead of keeping it between the ball and the side line.

TEACHING PROGRESSION

Blocking takes longer to teach and is more difficult to perfect than any other volleyball fundamental.

During the first workout, the coach should instruct his players on blocking techniques and include blocking drills in every practice session thereafter. All players should learn the techniques of the end and middle blocking positions to give the coach or captain the necessary flexibility to change blocking tactics during the course of a game. Constant individual attention during blocking drills is necessary since players are rarely aware of their mistakes while blocking.

When teaching the block, train the players in the important individual aspects before attempting to perfect the whole technique.

The following are some skills and drills for the coach to use in teaching blocking.

1. Administer the jump and reach test to determine what angle of knee flexion, armswing and approach each blocker should use.
2. Demonstrate; then have players practice the following:
    Slide step and jump
    Slide step and forward one-step approach that is to be used when blocking against taller opponents
    Slide step and diagonal one-step approach for blockers who are late in arriving at the proper blocking position
    Crossover step and jump (*Note:* Alternate to the right and left)
3. Lower net 2 ft.
    Explain and demonstrate the arm and hand position used to attack block, soft block, turn the ball in and close a hole between players to insure a tight block
    Line up players along the lowered net and have them practice various arm and hand positions.
4. Raise net to one foot under regulation height.
    Station two players facing each other on opposite sides of a lowered net. One player tosses the ball to himself and spikes it at two-thirds speed to the blocker who practices the correct hand and arm motion for the various blocks. The spiker progresses from hitting the ball at two-thirds speed to a predetermined area to hitting the ball at full speed, attempting to drive it by the blocker.
    Add a middle blocker and emphasize turning the ball in and coordinating a tight block. The spiker should hit the ball from various angles and depths in the court.
5. Have two players face each other on opposite sides of a regulation net.
    One player simulates a spiking motion while the blocker reaches over the net and attempts to touch the spiker's fingertips.
6. Place a spiker on a 2-ft. high bench. He tosses the ball up and spikes it at the blocker. The blocker practices the attack block, soft block and turning the ball in. Add a middle blocker and coordinate a tight block.
7. Have two players face each other on opposite sides of the net about 3 ft. apart. The spiker tosses the ball to himself and jumps straight up to hit it over the net. The blocker uses a slide step to intercept the spike.
8. Pair players of approximate height in two lines on each side of the net. Partners jump and touch hands above the net on the end, middle and other end of the net. Emphasize a fast slide step and maximum jump. Change the drill by having one player swing his spiking arm as he jumps. His partner must move his arms and hands to intercept the mock spike. Repeat the drill, using the crossover step.
9. Place two benches close to the net, about 3 ft. from the side line. Place a third bench near the center of the net. A spiker stands on each bench

and tosses the ball up and spikes it in rotation as the blocker moves from spiker to spiker using the slide or crossover step. To increase the difficulty of this drill, take away the benches and substitute three lines of spikers hitting in rotation to the single blocker.

GAME SITUATION DRILLS

After the blocker has developed a blocking style that suits his coordination, agility, jump and reach, he must participate in drills that simulate game situations.

It will take a good athlete about three years to be able to read the intentions of opposing spikers in top competition. Most players in open competition are still learning after they have passed the peak of their physical ability.

1. The spiker passes the ball to a setter, who delivers a high, wide set. The blocker attempts to cut off his strongest shot or block the ball. One-on-one blocking situations are becoming more common each year, as more teams switch to a three-hitter attack to set up a one-on-one play. Better spikers can usually beat a one-man block. Emphasize taking away the spiker's favorite angle or the best percentage shot for the particular set and approach used by the spiker.

2. Three blockers defend against two hitters. Station the spikers on the end of the net with the setter in the middle. Emphasize a tight, two-man block, with the off-blocker dropping back to the 10-ft. line to dig a spike driven inside the middle blocker.

3. Three blockers vs. three attackers. Emphasize that the middle blocker stay tight to the net if he is late and that individual blockers take the percentage spiking angles on one-on-one situations.

4. Three blockers vs. three attackers. The center spiker hits a quick, low set close to the net, and the outside spikers hit a normal set. Emphasize that the primary responsibility of the middle blocker is the center spiker. Instruct him to jump with the middle spiker and to recover and attempt to soft block the end spiker if he is fast enough. If he is out of position to soft block, he should remain close to the net and out of the play.

5. Two end attackers vs. three blockers. The middle blocker deliberately moves in the wrong direction and attempts to recover and join the end blocker. Emphasize that the middle blocker keep his hands close to the net and that he soft block when late. The end blocker must take more of the cross court angle and attempt to help close the hole between blockers.

6. After the blocker returns to the floor, throw a ball to a teammate who delivers a set to the player. Emphasize that he quickly back off the net for a three-step spiking approach.

7. Station two players on opposite sides of the net. Toss a ball about 15 ft. high within a foot of either side of the net. The players must decide to spike or block the ball. Toss 50 percent of the balls so that they fall directly on top of the net. Emphasize aggressive attack blocking and the formation of a roof around the ball with the hands.

8. Instruct the setter to deliver sets outside the court so that the spiker must hit the ball cross court. Emphasize soft blocking by the end blocker so that he can turn the ball into the court. Instruct the middle spiker to leave a wide space between his hands so that he can cover more area above the net. Show him that the ball cannot go through his hands (unless he leaves an extremely wide space) because of the angle of the ball's flight.

9. Construct blocking drills patterned to stop the attack of your chief opponent. Instruct the second team to simulate the opposition's attack to familiarize your blockers with their patterns.

7

Individual Defensive Technique

When the rules were changed to allow blockers to reach over the net, the status of the quickly reacting player who could "dig" or pass his opponent's spike became elevated. Aggressive blockers forced opposing setters to deliver the set 3–5 ft. away from the net so that spikers could avoid the block; consequently, the backcourt defensive player no longer had to defend against "straight-down" spikes and could have more time to react to the spike.

Fig. 7.1 Going to the Floor *If they hope to excel, players must accept this responsibility. Using this approach to dig hard-to-reach balls is as basic to the modern game of volleyball as the spike.* (Bud Fields)

Fig. 7.2 Digger's Stance *A low, defensive position affords both lateral and forward ping forward when the ball is contacted, quick lateral movements are difficult.*

Players who are not afraid to go to the floor to recover the attack have sufficiently increased their range of effectiveness to the extent that spikers rarely drive the ball directly to the floor.

STANCE

Diggers should be in a crouching position, feet spread further apart than shoulder-width to enable them to move laterally as well as forward. Body weight should be forward, with the digger leaning toward the spiker as he contacts the ball. Since hard spikes should be dug in an underhand position, hands should be held below the waist.

The forearm pass should be used whenever possible. This technique provides the best possible control of a hard-driven spike under current rule interpretations. The overhand pass of a hard spike is frequently called a "throw" by the official and is a poor percentage play.

The digger should use whatever stance is necessary to place the upper part of his body directly behind the oncoming ball. It is of little consequence whether the digger is in a balanced or unbalanced position, so long as he positions his body behind the ball to insure maximum accuracy at contact.

b

movement (No. 3). If a player's feet are closer than shoulder width apart or if he is step-
(Dr. Leonard Stallcup)

It takes many hours of intensive training for players to move instinctively in position for the best possible digging accuracy.

Slow-moving balls require the digger to move his arms toward the intended target area in order to provide the necessary momentum for the ball to travel the required distance.

Diggers can attain greater accuracy with slow-moving balls if they use the elbow lock pass to provide prolonged contact with the ball.

The digger often gives with, or "cushions," hard-driven spikes so that they do not rebound back over the net. This is accomplished when the digger falls backward in an off-balance position as he contacts the ball. After the dig, the player contacts the floor with his buttocks, small of the back and shoulders. Then he rocks forward to his feet. Arms and shoulders should move forward as feet touch the floor to assume a standing position.

A far more effective but little known technique for fielding hard spikes is the *high dig*. Players who use this technique are taught to move toward the oncoming ball and to contact it while their legs move up from a low squatting position. Arms are held parallel to the floor whenever the flight of ball permits, to enable the dig to travel high in the air on the digger's side of the net. Since the dig travels upward rather than forward, the player never has to cushion the ball. The player also has significantly greater body control.

Fig. 7.3 Forearm Pass *Toshi Toyoda contacts the ball with the interior part of his forearm, close to his wrist. Elbows are fully extended.* (Ealing Corp.)

Fig. 7.4 Move Behind the Ball *Player No. 9 will contact the ball just before his buttocks touch the floor.* (a). *In b, the player has gone to one knee to use the forearm pass.* (Dr. Leonard Stallcup)

a

b

a

b

Fig. 7.5 Digging Off-Speed Shots *Olympian Barbara Perry contacts the ball, even though it was necessary to move into an off-balance position to get behind it.* (Dr. Leonard Stallcup)

c

Fig. 7.6 Cushioning the Spike *The digger does not follow through with arms or body, but contacts the ball as he falls backward in an unbalanced position.* (Dr. Leonard Stallcup)

a

b

Fig. 7.7 High Dig *This eliminates the most frequent digging error: passing the spike back into the opponents' court.* (Los Angeles City Unified School District)

ONE-ARM DIG

The one-arm dig is quite common and is usually used to increase the lateral range of the defender. It should be used only when the ball is out of effective range for the two-hand forearm pass. The ball can be effectively contacted anywhere from the knuckles of the closed fist to the elbow joint. Beginning players should be instructed to contact the ball in the middle of the forearm. If they misjudge the ball and contact it higher on the forearm or lower on the hand, they will not misdirect the pass altogether.

Fig. 7.8 One-Arm Dig *This is often used to back up the spiker and pass block rebounds. The opposite arm extends in the other direction for better body control.* (Dr. Leonard Stallcup)

The heel of the hand and knuckles provide a good rebounding surface for hard-to-reach balls that require full arm extension.

Once the players learn to land on the floor without absorbing the force of impact on their head, wrist, elbow or knee, they should be run through vigorous digging drills which require them to leave their feet while fully concentrating on the flight of the ball.

The player should learn to roll to the floor when his body is placed in an off-balance lateral position. This technique allows the force of the fall to be absorbed by a large area of the body rather than letting the wrist or knee joint absorb the shock.

Fig. 7.12 shows sequence shots of the dig and roll. The digger takes a wide step sideways with the right leg as her left leg extends in an attempt to position her body behind the ball (*a*). Upon contact, she is already low to the ground (*b*). After the ball is hit (*c*), her buttocks, back and left shoulder contact the ground as knees bend (*d*). The player's body continues to roll over as the legs remain bent (*e*). As her toes contact the ground, she pushes her body to an upright position with her hands (*e,f*).

a

b

c

Fig. 7.9 Forearm   Contact   *The   interior
part of the forearm should be turned toward
the ball. Beginners often swing the arm in a
strictly vertical plane, which may cause the
ball to rebound backward.* (Los Angeles City
Unified School District)

a

b

c

Fig. 7.10 Hand Contact *Hand contact is used when the ball is hard to reach, or when the player wishes to pass the ball a greater distance. (*Ealing Corp.*)*

Fig. 7.11 Eyes on the Ball *Before concentrating on the approaching ball, players must be confident in their ability to fall without injury.* (Dr. Leonard Stallcup)

d

e

f

g

Fig. 7.12 Dig and Roll *The digger positions herself and hits the ball. She then rolls to a standing position.* (Gary Adams)

OVERHAND DIG

Current rule interpretations discourage using the overhand pass to dig a hard-driven spike. Some officials are in the habit of calling every overhand pass of a hard-driven spike a thrown ball. Since the overhand dig is a poor percentage play, coaches have instructed their diggers to stay deeper in the court so that spiked balls above their waist may travel out of bounds. This means that the diggers can keep their weight forward to dive for balls in front of them, and keep their hands below the waist to use the forearm pass or one-arm dig to field spikes.

Fig. 7.13 Overhand Dig   *Although it is still recommended to control slow-moving balls, the overhand dig of a hard-driven spike has become nearly obsolete under current rule interpretations.* (Dr. Leonard Stallcup)

Off-speed spikes and dinks can be fielded in the overhand position, as officials are far more lenient on slow-moving balls. The player should move quickly in position behind the ball and intended target area. Fingers should be spread and cupped, wrists tilted back so the passer can see the ball above the back of his hands. The ball should be contacted above the forehead; knees and arms should extend simultaneously as the wrists straighten.

When an overhand dig of a hard-driven spike is attempted, the player must be positioned directly behind the ball or, most likely, the referee will call a throw. At the same time the player can achieve longer contact with the ball

Fig. 7.14 Advanced Technique *Olympian Sharon Peterson, best female digger in the country, gains maximum control by moving laterally behind the ball and falling backward to cushion the momentum of the spike.* (Bud Fields)

and consequently greater control by falling backward as the ball is dug. This technique is known as "cushioning" the spike and is recommended when digging hard-driven balls in the overhand position. During the mid-1960's it was popular among the better defensive players. However, because of the strict interpretation of a thrown ball when using the overhand dig, it is rarely used at present.

DIVING

Diving has become a common defensive technique. It is used to reach balls that cannot be passed accurately from a standing position. It is also an emergency play for recovering otherwise out-of-reach balls. The ball can be contacted while one foot is still on the ground or while the entire body is in the air. The height of the dive depends upon height, distance and speed of the oncoming ball.

Many players prefer to play the ball with the back of their hand, particularly when digging a ball close to the floor. This *backhand dig* technique enables the player to keep his palms close to the floor in anticipation of a quick landing.

The higher the body is in the air, the harder it falls to the ground. In landing from this position, it is important to try and absorb the shock with as

Fig. 7.15 Low Dive *The digger stays low to the ground and often uses the back of the hand. For easier landing, the palm is toward the floor.* (Dr. Leonard Stallcup)

a

Fig. 7.16 Backhand Dig *Palms are directed toward the floor before contact. This adds valuable inches to an effective digging range. To bump the ball high into the air, the player usually must flick his wrist upward.*

b

c

d

Fig. 7.17 High Dive *George Sorentos makes an all-out high diving save.* (Bud Fields)

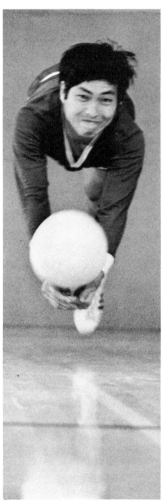

a

b

c

d

f

e

Fig. 7.18 Front Dive *Toshi Toyoda demonstrates the front dive.*

much body surface as possible. The momentum should not be stopped by the arms—rather, absorbed by the arms, chest and stomach in that order. Since the movement is usually downward rather than forward, there is little opportunity to slide. Players with poor arm strength will absorb the fall in a jolting bounce.

When diving parallel to the net, it is very difficult to use the two-hand forearm pass and recover in time for a safe landing. Therefore, the one-arm pass is recommended.

In Fig. 7.18, Toshi Toyoda crouches before taking the last step. His arms are in front while his forward foot pushes vigorously off the floor. His thrusting leg moves forward horizontally. He contacts the ball (forearm pass) and then rotates his palms toward the floor in preparation for the landing. As he descends, legs and feet are higher than his waist, his back is arched and

a

b

c

Fig. 7.19   Left-Hand Dig

head is up. Both arms are extended to contact the floor with both hands. To prevent violent contact with the floor, his body is arched correctly, his knees above his waist. His chest, stomach and, finally, legs must now contact the floor and the body will spend the momentum by sliding along the floor.

If the ball is traveling slowly, the player must swing his arm across his body to direct it to the intended target area (Fig. 7.19a, b). When digging a hard-spiked ball, the player should merely extend his arm.

Fig. 7.19 shows the left-hand dig. The dive to the left should receive a great deal of attention in practice sessions, as most players dig poorly when they must dive to their left.

BODY POSITION

Defensive strategy currently calls for backcourt players to remain near the side line and end line so that they will not have to dig hard-driven spikes in an overhand position. Hard spikes that are above a digger's waist are usually allowed to travel out of bounds. Therefore, the digger's basic position is a semi-squat in a wide stance (feet slightly more than shoulder-width apart), body leaning forward. This position affords quick lateral or forward movement. When expecting a hard spike, the player's hands should be held in an underhand position so that they can be joined together quickly for a fore-arm pass.

Often it is necessary for a player to assume a full squatting position to dig low balls. A wide stance should be used to maintain a controlled body position.

a

b

Fig. 7.20 Lateral Recovery *The digger protects his knees by arching his body after contact. He must keep his neck arched upward to prevent his chin from contacting the floor.* (Ealing Corp.)

Fig. 7.21 Basic Position *The digger's basic position is semi-squat, body leaning forward. Hands should be below the waist in anticipation of an underhand pass.* (Los Angeles City Unified School District)

MOVING TO THE BALL

Rather than merely reach for it with their arms, players should always strive to step toward the oncoming ball if time allows. As shown in Fig. 7.22, the low squatting position is used. American players are somewhat unaccustomed to the *low squatting position* and require hours of repetitive drills in the low position until movement becomes automatic. A common error is to keep the legs extended and to bend from the waist.

Fig. 7.22 Low Body Position *1964 Olympic captain Jane Ward demonstrates good balance with the center of her body above her back foot.* (Dr. Leonard Stallcup)

Fig. 7.23 Moving Laterally *Sharon Peterson positions herself behind the ball. The deeper player should call for the ball, since she can see both the position of her teammates and the ball at the same time.* (Bud Fields)

The slide step used in volleyball is similar to the defensive step in basketball. The outside foot points in the direction of movement and the other foot quickly draws even with the first. Since legs never cross, the player always faces the ball. When the player must cover the required distance in a short period of time, a lateral or forward lean of the body and roll may have to be added to the slide step so that he can get directly behind the ball for maximum passing accuracy.

The roll is used to prevent injuries and to return the player quickly to his feet. The ball is usually contacted just before thigh and buttocks hit the floor. After the buttocks contact the floor, the body continues to roll so that first the entire upper back, forward shoulder, knees and toes contact the floor as legs remain bent. The other foot contacts the floor as the player's hands push his body to an upright position. If the player contacts the floor too hard or too fast, he usually has not gradually lowered his body prior to contact. To protect his head, the player's back must remain arched and his chin should remain tucked against his chest during the entire roll.

When speed is needed for covering a large area of the court, one should turn and run, taking short, fast steps. The player should gradually lower his body to the height of the ball as he moves. If contact is made in an off-balance position, it is advisable to dive rather than risk an uncontrolled fall to the floor.

Fig. 7.24 Full Roll   *A well-executed roll is a safe conclusion to off-balance lateral movement.* (Dr. Leonard Stallcup)

Fig. 7.25 Run and Dive   *The dive is also recommended to recover from balance lateral movement.* (Dr. Leonard Stallcup)

LEARNING THE DIVE

Players should not attempt the dive until adequate arm strength is developed. Many women do not have adequate arm strength to slow their landing and, consequently, hit the floor on their chin. Push-ups will develop the necessary arm strength to slow the body's fall to the floor. If a player cannot support his body on outstretched arms and hands while another player holds his feet off the floor in a horizontal position, he is not strong enough to learn the dive.

Fig. 7.26 Learning the Dive   *When the player can arch his body and protect his knees, he should practice the long low dive for distant balls close to the mat.*

First, the player lies face down on a mat and arches his body so that knees and feet are higher than his waist. Next, his partner holds his feet while he extends his arms and lowers his body to the mat. Then the player kneels and falls forward, pushing against the mat as his arms flex.

Repeat the action from a standing position. Move off the mat to the floor, while instructing the player to fall forward from a standing position, and slide forward—chest touching the floor. Return to the mat and dive forward from a squatting position. Take a two-step approach and dive forward. Finally, lob a ball to the player who executes a diving save.

When a player learns the correct technique of diving without the ball, he is ready to progress to the backhand dig on the mat. In the beginning the coach or partner should lob the ball in a controlled manner and then gradually increase the distance and speed as progress is made. Beginners should

Fig. 7.27 Pepper Drill   *Pepper drills should be
included in every practice session.*

be encouraged to field high balls, thereby preventing the common tendency
of falling forward and striking the mat, knees first.

A pepper drill can be utilized to practice the dig. A coach or partner can
stand at distances of 10–30 ft. and alternate hard-driven spikes with off-
speed shots and dinks directed at the digger and just out of his reach. The
digger dives, rolls and makes whatever movements are called for according
to the height, direction and speed of the ball.

When the player is learning correct techniques, the coach should frequently stop the drill and comment on player execution. After technique is mastered, emphasis should be on many repetitions involving diving and rolling
saves. When a player automatically goes to the floor to dig the ball without
any hesitation, the necessary conditioned reflex for competition has been
formed.

Players should also receive plenty of instruction at each defensive court
position they will be required to play. The coach can stand on a table and
attack from various positions along the net to simulate game conditions.

Other players can retrieve balls and form a supply line to the coach so
that drill never has to slow down for lack of a ball. This concentrated digging
drill can send the player to the floor numerous times within a short period.
If repeated often enough, techniques such as diving and rolling saves will
become conditioned reflexes.

When individual techniques have been covered, players must learn their
team defensive responsibilities. The coach can use the table spike technique
against three backcourt players and an off-blocker. Once defensive responsibilities are learned, two blockers can be added to field a full defensive
team. Finally, the defensive team should practice against a live offense.

Part III

TEAM PLAY

(Bob Van Wagner)

8

Offense

Selection of a two- or three-hitter attack should depend on the limitations and strengths of the personnel. A simple two-hitter offense with few options would be the right selection for the overwhelming majority of college and open teams. When a team has four spikers who can hit a high, wide set reasonably well, there is usually little tactical reason to install a three-hitter attack.

During the last few years, the majority of college and open teams have switched to the three-hitter offense. These teams often attempt advanced plays and options which lead to excessive errors.

The great variety inherent in this three-hitter attack will be successful only if the players have the ability and practice time necessary to keep errors at a minimum. It is far better to master the simple two-hitter attack than to be fairly good at the more difficult three-hitter offense.

The offense attempts to hit the ball over the net in such a manner that the defense cannot return it. The normal offensive pattern calls for the ball to be passed close to the net to a setter; the setter then delivers the ball to a spiker to hit into the opponents' court.

TWO-HITTER ATTACK

The basic offensive alignment is the *four-two*. The four-two uses four players (*spikers* or hitters), who are responsible for hitting the ball over the net, and two players (*setters*), who are responsible for setting the ball to the spiker.

Fig. 8.1 Fundamental Offensive Technique *No. 9 receives the serve using the forearm pass (a). No. 22 follows through after setting the spiker (b). No. 11 spikes the ball as his opponent tries to block the attack (c).* (Bud Fields)

M-FORMATION

The **M**-formation, setter in the middle front, is the first formation that beginning players should learn. Many teachers require each player to set when he rotates to the middle front position; this gives everyone an opportunity to develop ball handling skills.

In Fig. 8.2, the setter is in the middle front, ready to receive a short serve that would barely clear the net. The five remaining players have lined up in a receiving formation that resembles the letter "M." The set should travel in an arc at a height of 4–10 ft. above the net and drop about 2 ft. from the net at the outside right or left front corner of the net.

Fig. 8.2 M-Formation *(setter in middle front) These junior high school girls have learned to receive the underhand serve using the overhand pass.* (Los Angeles City Unified School District)

a

b

Fig. 8.3 Set *A high pass drops in the center of the court within 2-4 ft. of the net (a). The setter runs and places the set high in the air, allowing the spiker to attack with maximum force.* (Los Angeles City Unified School District)

Setter Switch

When the front row setter rotates to an outside position, he must switch to the center after the serve so that he is in position to receive the pass. The switch starts as soon as the ball is served; the setter can remain in this position until the ball is dead. Before the next serve, the setter must return to his original position.

Fig. 8.4 Setter in His Right Front   (M-*Formation*) *The team's two best ball handlers are setters. They stand diagonally opposite one another so that one setter is always in the front row.*

In Fig. 8.4, the setter is in the right front position. He should start about 5 ft. from the side line to allow the spiker on the right to maintain a normal position for formation (Fig. 8.5). The rest of the players line up in an **M**-formation as they did when the setter was in the middle.

When the front row setter rotates to an outside position (Fig. 8.5), a switch to the center of the court should be made to put the setter in a better position to set either spiker (*b, c*). The "switch" is started as soon as the ball is contacted for the serve. The setter must return to the original position in the rotation before the next serve.

The two setters line up diagonally opposite each other, as do the two best spikers, so that one will always be in the front row. As basic fundamentals are learned and as skill and experience increase, the strongest spikers become apparent.

As the setter switches into the middle, one of the spikers must switch with the setter to the outside. If the best spikers are lined up so that they precede a setter in the service order, they should switch so that they hit twice from their on-hand, or left front, side (right-handed spiker). In Fig. 8.5 *b*, hitter No. 4, who is left front, spikes from the on-hand side as setter No. 2 switches into the center. In Fig. 8.5 *c*, after rotation of setter No. 2 to the back row, the other setter (No. 5) comes to the net. Hitter No. 4 now switches with the setter next to him and hits for the second time from the left front position. A left-handed spiker should line up so that he hits twice from his on-hand, or right, side.

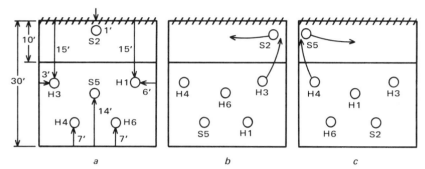

a   *b*   *c*

Fig. 8.5 Setter Switch   *The setter is in the middle (a); on the right (b); on the left (c).*

There is no need to switch when the setters rotate to the middle of the court. The front spikers pull back off the net to about center court, with the left front player very near the left side line and right front player crowding toward the center of the court toward the side from which the opponents are serving. The center back player is in the center of the court, even with or slightly behind the front row spikers, in order to cover the area vacated by the setter who is at the net. The left and right back players stand between the front row players, about 7 ft. from the back line.

Facing the Stronger Hitter

If one of the two spikers is significantly stronger than the other, the setter in the middle front rotation may move to the opposite side of the court and face the stronger player. Since forward sets are usually delivered with greater accuracy than over-the-head or back sets, this tactic allows the setter to use the percentage play. Since the setter is still in the middle front position, he may not overlap the right front spiker.

Backing Up the Passer

When the ball is served, at least one player should back up the passer. If the ball is served to the middle front as in Fig. 8.7, the player behind him moves directly in line with the serve in the event the front court player decides to let the ball go by him. The other backcourt player stands deep in

Fig. 8.6 Facing the Strongest Spiker *By moving as far to the side of the court as possible without overlapping the off-hand spiker's position, the setter can deliver a larger percentage of sets to his on-hand spiker.*

Fig. 8.7 Backing Up the Passer *Kirk Kilgour is shown backing up Dane Holtzman.*

the event the ball rebounds backward. Spikers do not begin their approach until they see that the pass will reach the setter. In the event of a bad pass, all five players must be ready to step in and set the ball to one of the front corners.

The player in the back row should tell the front row receiver whether to pass the ball or let it go by. The back row passer must judge accurately the height and speed of the serve while evaluating the ability of his front court teammate to pass the ball. Even though he calls for another player to receive the serve, the backcourt player should always be in a direct line with the ball in the event of a mix-up in signals.

Backing Up the Spiker

After the set, all players back up the spiker to handle *block rebounds*. This means covering the spiker in case the ball rebounds off the blocker's hands back into their court.

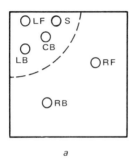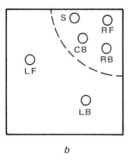

Fig. 8.8 Four-Two Spiker Coverage *This should be stressed constantly during practice. a shows a set to the left front; b, a set to the right front.*

a   *b*

If the ball is set to the left front spiker, the setter and other players move quickly in unison to a designated area. The left back comes in behind the spiker down the line from about 2–5 ft. behind the spiker—depending on how close the set is to the net and the ability of the opposing blockers. The center back man comes in the same distance behind the spiker, between the left back and setter. The setter completes the half-circle which surrounds the spiker, by being about 2–3 ft. from the net. The right front player pulls back off the net toward the rear of the court, and the right back moves toward the center of the court to the left side near the base line; both are then ready for a ball hit off the block.

If the set is to the right front player, the coverage is exactly the same on the opposite side of the court. If the ball is set within 18 in. of the net against aggressive blockers, the back-up players should crowd very close to the spiker in anticipation of the ball being blocked straight down. This tactic is not necessary against a small or poor block.[1]

Once the players reach their assigned positions they should stay low to the floor, arms outstretched and weight forward. Even All-American performers sometimes lose their concentration and watch the play. The key to backing up the spiker is *staying low* to give a player more time and distance to react to the block.

THREE-HITTER ATTACK

In the three-hitter attack, all six players can spike. Two spikers are designated as setter-hitters because of their superior ball handling ability. The three players at the net spike and a back row player sets. This formation offers skilled players an opportunity for multiple offensive plays. Most teams participating in international competition use a three-hitter attack. Since all three players in the front row become spikers, the player who cannot spike adequately usually becomes a backcourt substitute.

Coaches find that players prefer this type of offense over the slower four-two attack. It keeps the team moving constantly and provides a real challenge to players and coaches. Its obvious spectator appeal does much to popularize the sport wherever the offense is introduced. If the offense is executed correctly, spikers will have an opportunity to hit the ball with only one blocker to cope with.

In the United States, most collegiate and open teams do not fully understand the principles of defending against a sophisticated three-hitter attack. Opponents who are still using the four-two system find that they have to devote a good portion of valuable practice time to stopping the three-hitter offense rather than to perfecting their own fundamentals.

The Pass

The attack usually functions in direct relationship to the accuracy of the first pass.

Longer practices and concentrated individual and team passing drills are needed to perfect passing techniques. Since there is a great deal more movement in this system, physical and mental endurance must be built and maintained at a high level. A poorly conditioned team may get by using the two-hitter system, whereas the timing and pinpoint passing required in the three-hitter attack cannot be maintained in long matches and tournaments by poorly conditioned athletes.

Since the poor pass in this system destroys the offensive patterns by forcing the weaker ball handlers to set and the weaker spikers to hit, it is not always beneficial to run this offense against a strong serving team. If a team is continually forced into the four-two system by bad passes, it is better to play a straight four-two on the serve reception and allow the best ball handlers to set the best hitters. A team may elect to use the three-hitter attack only on the "free ball," when it can be passed accurately.

On-Hand Spiking

If the ball is passed within 5 ft. of the net and approximately 8–12 ft. from the right side line, the setter can easily deliver a front set to either the left or center front spikers, who will approach the set from their advantageous on-hand side.

a   *b*

Fig. 8.9 Setter Facing the Middle and Left Front Spiker *With a flick of his wrists Olympic setter Pedro Velasco can deliver the ball to either spiker (a). The Japanese National Team (b) uses this system.* (Dr. Leonard Stallcup)

Right-handed spikers have an excellent opportunity to boost their spiking efficiency since they are approaching the set from their strongest side in two out of three rotations. The off-hand spiker, who approaches from behind the setter in the right front, is often relatively ignored by the blockers and can often hit a wide back set unopposed. In Fig. 8.10 the blockers have concentrated on No. 10, the middle spiker leaving No. 13 without a blocker.

Back Row Setter

In the three-hitter attack, the setter always comes from the back row. Most teams only have two players who are capable of setting, and they are placed diagonally opposite each other with the assignment of setting in each of the three back row positions. When the setter is in the left back position, it is

Fig. 8.10 Back Set to the Open Spiker *Toshi Toyoda has sensed the presence of the blockers and delivers a back set to the open spiker, Kirk Kilgour (No. 13).* (Bob Van Wagner)

difficult for him to run in across the court to the right of center, turn and face the two on-hand hitters and set the ball.

This is the only position in which it may be necessary to let the right back player handle the setting. If this is the case, the player preceding the setter in the serving rotation (called the *technique player*) must be a good ball handler. Technique players must be diagonally opposite one another so that one always plays the right back when the setter is left back. The addition of the

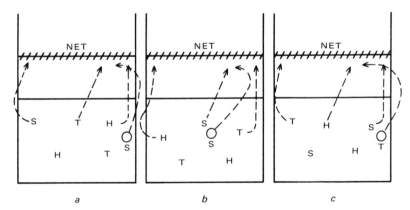

Fig. 8.11 Three-Hitter Offense *H—hitter, S—setter, T—technique, O—player who sets the ball. a shows a setter in the right back; b, a setter in the middle back; c, a technique setter in the right back.*

technique players eliminates the most vulnerable service receiving position of the *six-two* system because the setter now has a shorter distance to travel to receive the pass.

The best formation for the six-two offense is as follows: the two best hitters stand diagonally opposite each other; the technique player and setters stand opposite each other. In Fig. 8.11 *c*, the technique player (right back) moves from the right side line to the passing area in the right side of the court. If the setter moves from the left side line, his team may become vulnerable to fast side line serves directed in his path. These three rotations are sound, fundamental receiving positions for the three-hitter attack. The basic pattern of the six-two is to pass the ball to the setter in the right front center of the court, who comes in from the back row.

Serve Reception

In lining up to receive the serve, the three front players pull back off the net to about midcourt.

The left front stays near the left side line, and the right front moves near the side line toward the opponents' server. The middle front stands between these players. The setter in the middle back is shielded from the serve by the middle front player (Fig. 8.12 *a*). The left and right back play about 6 ft. behind and between the front row players. In the next rotation the line-up is the same, except that the setter or technique player hides behind the right front player.

Fig. 8.12 Setter Moving from the Middle Back   *No. 9 moves toward his target area as the server contacts the ball (a). All five players watch the passer in case they must set an inaccurately passed ball (b).*

a

b

Play Sets

The six-two or three-hitter attack effectively lends itself to the use of play sets, which normally create numerous instances of one ill-positioned blocker defending against the spiker. A team should be given the freedom to call its own sets or plays as it sees fit. If the coach tells his players to use only certain sets and plays in particular situations, the opposition would soon be able to predict the attack. Spikers or setters may call for a play at any time during the course of a game, either before or after the serve.

Play sets are automatically called off if the primary setter cannot reach the pass; otherwise, the spiker or spikers are totally committed to the play. The setter makes the final decision whether to deliver the play set or to set a normal ball to another spiker. One spiker should expect a normal set in the event the pass is not accurate enough to deliver the play set.

Four basic play sets have enabled setters to create favorable attack conditions: the one-set, two-set, three-set and four-set. It is not necessary for a spiker to be secretive when calling for these sets, since the setter has the option of delivering the ball to the other two spikers if the defense stacks its block on one player.

The most exciting offensive play in volleyball is the well-executed spike of an extemely low set placed only a foot or so above the net. *Spiking the*

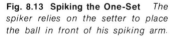

Fig. 8.13 Spiking the One-Set *The spiker relies on the setter to place the ball in front of his spiking arm.*

one-set has become a common play in the three-hitter attack. The Japanese perfected this play to defeat the block of their taller opponents by utilizing split-second timing between spiker and setter.

The spiker moves to within a few feet of the setter when he is moving into position to receive an accurate pass. The setter must gauge the spiker's approach while watching the descending pass. If the spiker is late, the setter must drop to a squatting position before contacting the ball to give the spiker time to jump. If the spiker is early, the setter must extend his arms to set the ball as quickly as possible. He should be at the top of his jump just as the ball is clearing the tape.

If the blocker jumps with the spiker, the setter may set to another player; if the blocker does not jump, the spiker has an easy chance to put the ball on the floor. If the pass is more than a few feet from the net, the setter must put more force on the *one-set* and deliver it toward the spiker at the net. If the spiker mistimes his approach, the set will often cross the net. The middle spiker automatically prepares to hit this "one-shoot" instead of the normal straight up and down one if the pass is off the mark.

The *two-set* usually travels from 2–4 ft. above the net. It does not require the same split-second timing as the Japanese set and can be mastered by any good spiker. Because of the extra height on the set, the spiker usually has at least one blocker defending against the play. Although the approach

Fig. 8.14 Middle Spiker Hitting a Two-Set *The two-set travels 2-4 ft. above the net and is often contacted on its downward flight. This play is usually quick enough to prevent two blockers from forming in front of the spiker.* (Bud Fields)

is nearly completed before the setter touches the ball, the spiker does not jump until after the setter contacts the ball; the ball is usually hit on its downward flight.

The *three-set* is placed about 10 ft. from the left side line. It is delivered low and fast to the middle spiker. The ball should not reach a height of more than 2 ft. above the net. The three-set is designed to beat a slow middle blocker and to isolate the off-hand spiker in a one-on-one blocking situation.

The "shoot," or *four-set*, is placed about a foot from the side line, at a height of 1–2 ft. above the net. The play is very difficult for the middle blocker to cover when the ball travels a distance of 15–20 ft. from setter to spiker. The middle blocker will invariably be late on the block, usually leaving the cross court area open for a hard-driven spike.

In the three-hitter system, the jump set is used effectively by the front row player, who reacts with split-second timing to the opposing block. If the blocker does not jump with the setter, the setter spikes the ball; if the blocker does jump, he sets the ball and creates a none-on-one or one-on-one blocking situation. The jump set is also utilized by backcourt setters to confuse the block.

Backing Up the Spiker

When backing up the hitter in this system, the two spikers who do not receive the set and the setter from the back row must move quickly to form the semicircle around the hitter.

Fig. 8.15 Spiking a Jump Set *No. 1 continues upward after the ball is hit out of his fingertips. The opposition's blocker arrives a split second too late to block the spike.*

Fig. 8.16 Forming a Semi-Circle to Back Up the Spiker *Mike Bright (left) is one of the three players backing up the spiker. Notice Mike's low body position and balance.*

The depth of the three front players supporting the spiker depends on the closeness of the set, the ability of the opposing blockers and the spiking habits of the attacker. Attackers who hit low tend to be blocked straight down and require the supporting players to move close to the net in a low position. Small blockers tend to softly block the ball deep into the attackers' court; and, the supporting players should stay deeper.

The two players providing secondary coverage fill the gaps in between the front line players and cover the ball that rebounds deep in the court. The setter is the key player who moves into the area where most of the block

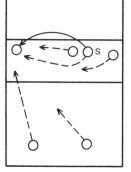 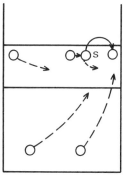

Fig. 8.17 Covering the Normal Set *a shows a set to the left front; b, a set to the right front.*

a   *b*

rebounds fall. They must be reminded to follow their set, particularly when setting over their heads.

In Fig. 8.17a, the ball is set to the left front spiker; the center front has approached and jumped for the fake set. The center front must now move quickly to assume the "back-up" position about 2–3 ft. from the net. The setter, in turn, must go around the center front spiker to get to the position behind the spiker, between the left back and center front. The remaining players back up the spiker as they would in the four-two system.

In Fig. 8.18a, the center spiker receives the set. The outside spikers must move in quickly to back up the hitter while the setter moves to get behind the hitter and between the two outside spikers. The two back row players are deep between the setter and outside spikers.

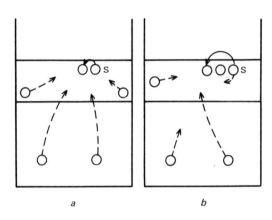

Fig. 8.18 Covering Play Sets *Supporting players must get close to the spiker, as blocked balls tend to rebound straight down (a). The right cross utilizes a two-set to the right front spiker, who moves behind the middle attacker (b).*

a   *b*

In Fig. 8.18b, the middle attacker is still in the air feigning a one-play when the ball is hit and is obviously out of the play. The setter steps toward the attacker as the left front and right back players form the rest of the semicircle. The left back player covers deep rounds off the block.

Player Qualifications

Setters must block and spike efficiently as well as deliver accurate sets. To take advantage of the three-hitter attack, they must master the four play sets. The setter must be a complete player. The only two Americans ever named to All World teams played the setter's position in a three-hitter attack.

Technique players set when they are in the right back position. Although mastery of the one- and three-sets is not necessary, the technique player should work toward delivering an adequate two- and four-set to complement the standard set. Since technique players are normally hitters first and setters by conversion, they should not attempt to become fancy when setting in crucial situations. During rallies, the technique man often comes to the front court to set, particularly if the setter is assigned the middle back position in the defense.

A strong quick *spiker* who is able to think and react when confronted with opposing blockers is essential. He should also be able to jump well in order to block the middle position in the front court rotations. After the block, he becomes the middle spiker during rallies and must develop a varied attack to get by the opposition's strongest blockers.

Advanced Patterns and Plays

Many different *serve reception patterns and plays* are used in the six-two attack, depending upon the personnel, playing rotation and the opponents' strength. If the middle front spiker is a good passer, but not quite fast enough to hit the one-set from a normal position, he can start from the spiking line 10 ft. from the net. When the middle front player is not a valuable passer, the four-man receiving pattern in Fig. 8.19*b* can be used.

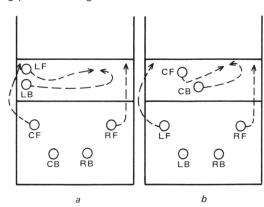

Fig. 8.19 Four-Man Receiving Pattern   *It is not necessary for the setter to run so far (a) when this is used. If the center front player is a poor passer, he should move under the net (b). Thus, he is taken out of the receiving pattern and may concentrate on the attack.*

Four-man receiving formations are very efficient if four superior passers are receiving the serve. Many outstanding national teams use four players to receive the serve. The advantage of this system is that the player approaching for the one-set has no serve-receiving responsibilities and can concentrate on the attack.

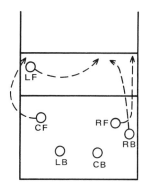

Fig. 8.20 Changing Attack Positions   *This can be easily accomplished when the players assume a four-man receiving pattern.*

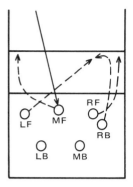

Fig. 8.21 Pass and Switch *Upon receiving the serve, the middle front player changes assignments with the left front spiker.*

It may be desirable to use the four-man receiving pattern when the setter is in the right back, if the left front spiker wants to switch attack positions with the center front spiker.

Coaches may elect to change attack assignments only when the middle front player receives the serve in the regular formation. Many middle spikers have great difficulty in passing the ball accurately and recovering to arrive at the point of attack in time for a quick one-set. By switching outside for a normal high set, they have time to concentrate fully on the accurate placement of their pass.

There are many other variations that can be used when the first pass is perfected. The cross, tandem and thirty-one are particularly effective when the opposition begins to stop the "one-play." These plays require a great deal of practice before timing is perfected.

If the blocker jumps with the first attacker, the setter has the option of delivering the ball to the right front spiker who crosses behind the middle attacker and jumps immediately after the first spiker. The second spiker can ask for a one- or two-set and approach off the first spiker's heels or the middle of the court. (See Fig. 8.22.)

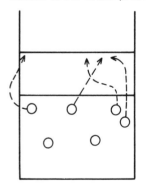

Fig. 8.22 Right Cross *The middle attacker approaches for the one-set and should receive it if the blocker remains on the floor.*

In Fig. 8.24, the spiker on the right should approach directly at the end blocker to hold him in position, and then abruptly change direction to cross in front of the setter to avoid the block.

Fig. 8.23 Tandum *The middle attacker approaches for the one-set hoping to draw the middle blocker while the setter delivers a two-set to the left front spiker jumping behind him.*

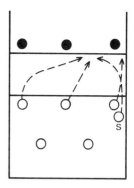

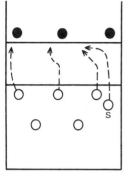

Fig. 8.24 Thirty-One *The middle attacker approaches to the left of center for a three-or shoot set, while the right front spiker crosses in front of the setter for a one-set.*

The *thirty-one* is particularly effective when the right spiker is left-handed and can spike a back one-set. The middle spiker runs in for a three-set to draw the middle blocker (No. 6, Fig. 8.25) in his direction as the right spiker approaches and jumps for the quick back set.

Fig. 8.25 Spiking the Back One-Set *This difficult play catches the block flat-footed. It is easier to execute if the spiker approaches from his on-hand side. If the spiker is late in his approach, the setter compensates by dropping to one knee to delay the set.* (Bob Van Wagner)

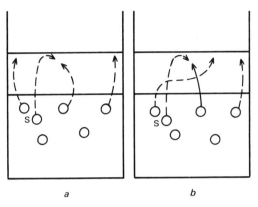

Fig. 8.26 Pass Left *The left-hander can spike from the middle position on the on-hand side (a). The left cross (b) can be added when opponents start keying on the one-play.*

a   b

When a left-handed spiker is in the middle front, the line-up shown in Fig. 8.26 can be used. This allows the middle attacker to spike the "one" on the power side—a maneuver that confuses the opponents' blocking patterns.

FIVE-ONE ATTACK

A five-one offense can add spiking and blocking power to the offense. If only one setter qualifies as one of the top six players on a team, this offense should be considered. The setter must be the type of athlete who can perform reliably during the entire contest. The entire offense bogs down as soon as the setter gets rattled.

When the setter is in the back court, this offense utilizes a three-hitter attack. When the setter rotates to the front row, a straight four-two or two-spiker attack is used.

The 1968 National Men's Champions changed to a five-one offense by replacing an outstanding 5-ft. 11-in. setter with a 6-ft. 7-in. spiker, in order to gain the additional blocking and spiking strength necessary for winning the match.

The Santa Monica YMCA also captured the 1971 title using this offense. They won the championship match rotating two different players in the setting position.

REFERENCE

1. Scates, Allen E., and Ward, Jane. 1969. *Volleyball*. Boston: Allyn and Bacon. See pp. 46 and 47.

9

Defense

The two basic defensive alignments used in power volleyball are the *middle back* and *middle in*. In both defenses, every player is assigned an area of the court which varies according to the set, block and intentions of the spiker.

STARTING POSITIONS

The individual's back court ready position is the same in all defenses. His body is in a semi-crouch position, feet spread about shoulder width apart. Weight is forward and hands are held about waist-high.

Players should assume the team starting position before changing into the middle back or middle in defense, so that their opponents cannot identify their alignments and attack the weak areas. The defense should remain in the team starting position until after the offense passes the serve. The traditional American defense is the middle back, whereas teams in other countries use variations of the middle back and middle in to meet the changing offensive tactics of their opponents.

MIDDLE BACK DEFENSE

The middle back defense is effective against teams that spike off the top and over the block without varying their attack with dinks and off-speed shots. When the opponents pass the serve, the defensive players should

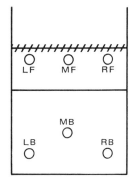

Fig. 9.1 Defensive Starting Position *Regardless of the defensive alignment that is used, the starting position for all defenses should be the same.*

move to their assigned areas of the court. The tactic of moving after the pass prevents the offense from readily observing the defensive alignment and hinders their attack on weak areas in a particular defense. The middle back defense is currently the most widely used defensive alignment at all levels of competition.

End Blocker

The end blocker should line up even with the spiker in this defense to block the line shot and encourage the spiker to hit cross court. The average back court defender on the side line directly in front of the attacking spiker must

Fig. 9.2 End Blocker Defending Against the Line Shot *Kim Meyers spikes into the end blocker.* (Dr. Leonard Stallcup)

move to within 15 ft. of the net when the ball is attacked, in order to field balls dinked over the block. When this defender rushes in to field the dink and the spiker drives a ball down the line, it is rarely dug. For this reason, it is often good strategy for the end blocker in the middle back defense to block the line and try to force the spiker to hit cross court. This defense is particularly strong against cross court spikes, since two defenders should always be outside of the middle blocker (LF, LB, Fig. 9.3)

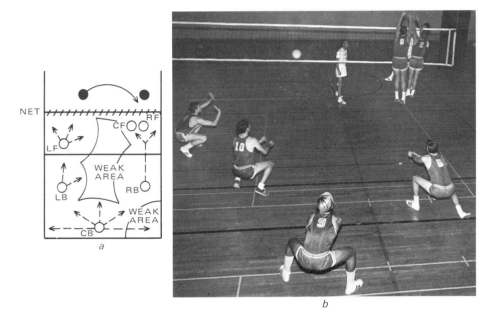

Fig. 9.3 Middle Back Defense *Two defenders (b)—Nos. 6 and 10—position themselves in the area of a cross court spike hit by the middle blocker.*

Off-Blocker

The off-the-net blocker (LF, Fig. 9.3) has moved about 9 ft. away from the net to field the spike driven sharply by the middle blocker. This player is also responsible for dinks and off-speed shots hit into the left side of the front court. The off-blocker must concentrate on moving away from the net quickly and stopping before the spiker contacts the ball. When the spiker contacts the ball, the off-blocker's body weight must be forward, or else he will not be able to move forward quickly enough to field balls hit off the block or to field soft placement shots.

The off-blocker must react quickly to the direction of the set in order to gain position deep enough in the court to dig the sharp spike angled by the block. The middle blocker who aggressively blocks over the net will force the setter to deliver the ball about 3 or 4 ft. from the net so that most spikers will not be capable of angling hard-driven cross court spikes inside the 10-ft. line. The off-blocker has a tendency to continue running back beyond the 10-ft. spiking line where he might overlap the left back player who usually has a much better angle on the approaching spike.

Left Back

The left back defender (No. 10, Fig. 9.3b) is stationed in the "power alley" of the volleyball court. Some coaches switch their best back court digger to this position because, most of the time, the average on-hand spiker will deliver the ball to this area of the court. This position is the key to backcourt defense because most teams set the on-hand spiker significantly more than the other hitters in both two- and three-hitter attacks. Number 10 in Fig. 9.3b has lined up off the center blocker's left shoulder so that he can watch the ball and spiker when making contact. He has moved forward and assumed a position low to the floor to dig a hard spike.

Middle Back

The middle back player (No. 9, Fig. 9.3b) is responsible for balls hit off the top or over the block. Many of the balls he fields are deflected by the block and can be set to one of the end blockers. In the traditional middle back defense, this player is not responsible for short dink shots.

The middle back must be ready to move forward when he sees that the blockers have not closed in fast enough and have left a hole in the middle of the block. When stationed behind a good block, this player should be in a direct line behind the blockers and attacking spiker. The middle back starts just inside the end line and moves in the direction of the spike. Setters often play this position, which is comparable to the free safety in football.

Right Back

Number 22 in Fig. 9.4 is playing the right back position. He is responsible for covering balls hit down the line as well as dinks and soft shots looped over the block. This position requires a player who has the ability to "read" the intentions of the opposing spiker. It is extremely difficult for him to recover a soft dink shot which drops at the heels of the blockers when he has ruled out that possibility and has moved close to the floor in preparation for a hard-driven spike. The initial starting position for this player is near the side line, about 10 ft. from the end line.

DEFENSING THE CENTER SPIKER

When the center spiker in a three-hitter offense receives a one-set, it is nearly impossible to defend the play with more than one blocker. The block-

Fig. 9.4 Right Back Defender *No. 22 prefers to play this position when using the three-hitter attack. It enables him to move quickly into setting position when the ball is dug.*

Fig. 9.5 Defending the Quick Set *Pedro Velasco (No. 5) blocks the middle position in all three front court rotations. He has outstanding jumping ability.* (Bob Van Wagner)

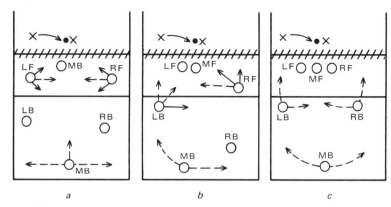

a   b   c

Fig. 9.6 Center Spiker Vs. the Middle Back Defense *Only the middle blocker can react in time to stop the quick one-set. If the left and right front players can move quickly, they can back off the net to field dink shots and block rebounds (a). The end blocker can easily join the middle blocker when a normal set is delivered to the middle attacker. Blockers with quick reactions may be able to join the middle blocker to stop a two-set. The end player, from whom the ball is set away, should block since most spikers have a habit of dinking the ball across their body (b). The other blocker drops off the net to dig a spike hit past the middle blocker and cover the dink shot. The three-man block should be used only to stop powerful spikers who rarely dink (c). The three-man block leaves too much area for the backcourt players to cover.*

er should normally attempt to stay in front of the spiker's attacking arm in an attempt to force him to cut the ball back across his body (No. 5, Fig. 9.5).

If time allows, the off-blockers (LF, RF, Fig. 9.6a) back off the net to cover dinks and balls deflected by the blocker. The corner back players (LB, RB, Fig. 9.6a) line up outside the blocker's arms so that they can see the spiker contact the ball. The center back player stays deep behind the blocker and reacts to the spike (MB, Fig. 9.6a). If the blocker does not jump in time, this player must run forward to dig the straight-ahead spike.

Two Blockers

Two blockers should defend against the center spiker unless the setter delivers a one- or three-set. Since most spikers consistently dink the ball in the direction of the set, the blocker on the right will cover the dink if the ball is set from the left and vice versa. The corner back player (LB, Fig. 9.6b) will approach the 10-ft. spiking line if the player in front of him is involved in the block.

Three Blockers

When the middle attacker receives a normal set, it is usually possible to defend with three blockers. This is not considered good strategy most of the time, however, because the three remaining backcourt players cannot cover the court adequately in the event of a dink or soft spike (Fig. 9.6c).

Fig. 9.7 Center Spiker Vs. Three-Man Block *It is good strategy to use a three-man block against a spiker who cannot often be stopped by two men.* (Bud Fields)

Using three blockers against an accomplished spiker who has been hitting well against a two-man block can be most effective. This three-man block is also valuable against players who cannot dink well or use a soft spike.

MIDDLE BACK DEFENSE TO OFFENSE

Two-Hitter Attack

If the digger does not pass the ball accurately when fielding the attack, one of the remaining five players who is closest to the pass should set the ball to one of the front row spikers. When the pass or dig can be controlled, the transition from the middle back defense to the two-hitter offense depends on the location of the setter.

Normally, the setter is not the strongest blocker in the front row and is not capable of blocking the middle position effectively. When a team has a tall, mobile setter who is talented enough to block the middle, its transition to offense becomes very smooth since there is no setter-spiker switch.

Setter Blocking Left

Since the attack usually comes from the opposition's on-hand spiker or strong side, the weak blocking setter usually switches to the left to block

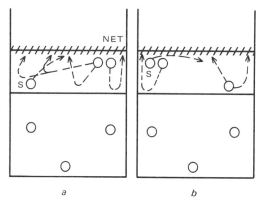

Fig. 9.8 Setter Blocking on the Left
If there is not enough time for the middle blocker to get to the left side of the court to approach from the on-hand side, the approach can be made from the middle of the court (a). If the attack is dug from the opponents' weak side, the middle blocker may approach easily along the side line (b).

a   b

the attack from the weak side. This allows the setter to become the off-blocker, having the responsibility of digging cross court spikes (S, Fig. 9.8*a*).

When a teammate digs a ball, the setter switches with the center blocker and sets to one of the front row players. This is the best system for defending against the opponents' attack, but is most inefficient for the middle blocker. The player who blocks the middle must use a shortened approach if he wants to reach the left front spiking position in time for the set. He may choose to attack from the middle by verbally signaling the setter while the first pass is in the air. A middle attack has the disadvantage of allowing the opposing blockers to cover 15 ft. of the net instead of 30 ft.; this means they should be able to block successfully with two or three players if they so desire. If the first pass is not high, the setter usually has his back to the on-hand spiker and is not sure of the location of the approaching spiker.

When the attack is from the weak side, the switch is relatively easy (S, Fig. 9.8*b*). The former off-blocker may approach for a play set since the setter is usually facing him.

Setter Blocking Right

If the setter is a strong end blocker, he should block the right side. When the attack is from the opponents' strong side, the center blocker can approach from the middle or use a short switch and approach from the right side. If the attack is from the weak side, the middle blocker should attack from the middle so that the set can be approached from the on-hand side.

The Russian team stationed its setters on the right side to block during recent world competition, even though their blockers were noticeably weaker than their spikers. Their diggers always passed the ball to the right side of the court to allow the setter to face two on-hand spikers, which allows greater accuracy in the placement of the set.

When the attack is dug from the opponents' strong side, the middle blocker can approach from the on-hand side in the middle or from the side line (Fig. 9.9*a*). When the attack is dug from the opponents' weak side, the middle blocker should approach from the middle of the court (Fig. 9.9*b*).

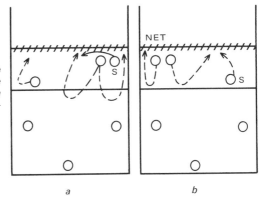

Fig. 9.9 Setter Blocking on the Right *When the setter is a capable blocker, it is good strategy to switch him to the right side for an easy transition to offense.*

NET

a   *b*

Down Block

Teams must be able to make quick adjustments from defense to offense. The serving team must anticipate a good pass, good set and then the spike. If the pass is not good and the setter has trouble getting to the ball, or if another player must step in and set the ball, the defense should be ready for a bad set. If the set is good enough to be hit by the spiker at a downward angle, but not sharp enough to block, the blockers yell, "Down!" or "Stay down!" At this call the blockers drop their arms and the off-blocker and three backcourt players attempt to dig the ball. When a backcourt player digs the ball, it should be directed to the front court setter.

Fig. 9.10 Down Block *When the spiker receives a set that must be hit deep into the defenders' court, "staying down" allows the diggers a clear view of the approaching ball.* (Dr. Leonard Stallcup)

Fig. 9.11 Free Ball *When a defender sees that the spiker is not likely to receive a good set, he should call, "Free!" Then, the blockers can drop off the net to help their backcourt teammates field the ball.* (Bud Fields)

Free Ball

When the defense sees that the offense will hit the ball over the net with an upward flight or weak spike, it should call, "Free!" and assume a normal serve reception pattern.

Three-Hitter Attack

The transition from the middle back defense to the three-hitter attack is a bit more complicated. If the defense does not pass the ball successfully when fielding the attack, it must use the two-hitter offense. When the back-

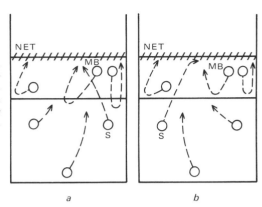

Fig. 9.12 Changing from the Middle Back Defense *The backcourt setter switches to the right side line (a). The setter switches to the left side line to allow the left-handed middle spiker to approach from the on-hand side (b).*

a   *b*

court setter digs the ball, he should direct it toward the front court setter and the team will use the conventional two-hitter attack. If another player digs the ball, it normally should be directed about 10 ft. from the right side line, a few feet from the net. The most convenient place for the backcourt setter to make a speedy transition to offense is the right back (S, Fig. 9.12*a*). With continued practice it is possible for the backcourt setter to move under a good dig from any defensive assignment, turn and face the two on-hand spikers and set the ball.

When the middle blocker is left-handed and a powerful spiker, the setter should play in the left back (S, Fig. 9.12*b*) and the dig should be directed a few feet from the net, about 10 ft. from the left side line. This allows the setter to play in the power alley, and the left-handed spiker can approach the set from the on-hand side. If a free ball is called, the backcourt setter runs to the net to give the diggers a target to pass to.

MIDDLE IN DEFENSE

The middle in defense is strong against dinks and off-speed hits. Teams with quick, tall blockers can prevent the opposition from attacking the weak zone that is located in the center of the court beyond the 10-ft. line.

The end blocker should line up about 3 ft. from the side line and move the block toward the center of the court in an attempt to encourage the spiker to hit the ball down the line.

If the ball is set near the side line and close to the net, the *end blocker* will have to line up on the ball to prevent a straight-down spike that cannot be dug by the defensive player on the line (RB, Fig. 9.13).

Right Back

The right back player is responsible for spikes hit down the line and for long balls hit off the block that fall on the right side of the court. The right back player does not take any responsibility for the short dink shot and can con-

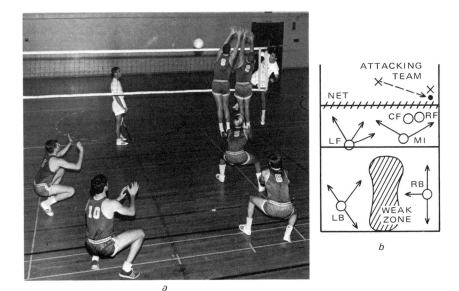

b

a

Fig. 9.13 Middle In Defense   *Teams are used to attacking the popular middle back defense and usually have difficulty adjusting to this defense.*

Fig. 9.14 End Blocker Encouraging Spiker to Hit a Line Shot   *The spiker accepts the invitation and slams the ball past the opponents' block.* (Dr. Leonard Stallcup)

Fig. 9.15 Right Back Stays Deep   *This player should concentrate on digging long spikes and not rush the net to dig the difficult "straight-down" spike.* (Dr. Leonard Stallcup)

Fig. 9.16 Protecting Against the Dink Shot   *No. 15 spikes as his opponent moves into position behind the blockers.* (Dr. Leonard Stallcup)

centrate fully on the spiker's line shots. If the right back is a good digger, the end-blocker should concentrate on the cross court spike and rely on the right back player to handle the line shot.

Middle In

Balls that are looped over the block are covered by the middle in player who started behind the center blocker on the 10-ft. line. The in player is not responsible for hard-driven spikes and concentrates on retrieving dinks, offspeed shots and block rebounds. He should be able to dive quickly to retrieve balls, and often becomes the setter when the team uses a three-hitter attack.

In Fig. 9.16, the middle in player must start on the 10-ft. line behind the blockers and concentrate on the possibility of a dink shot and his chances of retrieving balls rebounding off the block. If the spiker manages to drive a hard spike through the middle of the block, there is little possibility that the middle in player will field a successful dig at such a close distance.

Left Back

The left back player should be in line with the ball and armswing of the spiker. He should start about 5 ft. in from the end line and side line. Although his primary responsibility is digging spikes hit outside the blocker's left hand, the left back player is also responsible for balls hit over the block. He must have good lateral movement.

Fig. 9.17 Left Back Lining Up the Spike   *Shar Buhlig (No. 6) spikes a set delivered by Wendy Treffrey.* (Bud Fields)

In Fig. 9.17, No. 7 moves laterally to line up the spike traveling over the blocker's fingertips. Although no player is stationed directly behind the block in the middle in alignment, the better blockers will slow up the spike or force the spiker to hit in a flat trajectory to give the backcourt player time to dig the ball.

Off-Blocker

The off-blocker should quickly back off the net to the 10-ft. line while watching the setter and remaining blockers (Fig. 9.18a). When the ball is set toward the center of the court, he should move close to the side line. When the middle blocker does not jump or the set is wide, the off-blocker should move toward the center of the court (Fig. 9.18b).

Middle Blocker

The middle blocker is responsible for closing any spaces or holes in the block. Since there is no deep middle backcourt player, the middle blocker must slow up or block spikes hit in the center so that the backcourt players have time to move laterally to field the ball. The middle blocker usually pulls

b

a

Fig. 9.18 Off-Blocker Lining Up the Spike   *Barbara Perry is in a perfect position to dig a spike by Terri Condon. b* (Ealing Corp., *a*; Dr. Leonard Stallcup, *b*)

Fig. 9.19 Middle Blocker Letting the Dink Go By *The middle blocker drops his hands to allow the middle in player to field the dink shot.* (Bob Van Wagner)

his hands below the net if the spiker dinks, to allow the player behind the block to pass an easy ball.

In Fig. 9.19, the middle blocker should have shouted, "No!" or "Down!", thereby warning his teammate from deflecting the ball away from the middle in player. Notice the full squat of the player who is backing up the spiker. The outstanding male players on the Japanese National teams back up their spikers in this position. Squatting like this allows the player more time to react to a blocked ball.

STOPPING THE CENTER ATTACK

When a blocker finds himself alone on the block and defending himself against the middle spiker, he should cover the center of the court. This is particularly important in the middle in defense because there are no back-court players behind the block.

Fig. 9.20 Three-Set *The three-set often traps blockers at the net.* (Dr. Leonard Stallcup)

In Fig. 9.20, the blocker has found herself alone on the block and realizes that she must defend against the middle spiker. In this case, she must cover the center of the court. Teammates should remember that there are no backcourt players behind the block in the middle in defense.

The ideal court coverage for a one-player block is shown in Fig. 9.21a. Both off-blockers (LF, RF) drop off the net about 8 ft. to dig a spike hit toward the side line. The middle in player lines up off the blocker's right shoulder to cover dink shots. This player "cheats" to the right because most dink shots are placed in the same direction as the set. The backcourt players (LB,RB, Fig. 9.21a) line up off the outside shoulder of the blocker so that they can see the spiker contact the ball and then react to the attack.

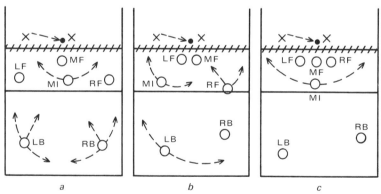

        a   *b*   *c*

Fig. 9.21 Center Spiker Vs. Middle In Defense *The middle in player should stay to the right of a one-man block when the set is coming toward him, since most spikers dink away from the direction of the set (a). When two players block the middle attacker, the middle in player must cover the area vacated by the end blocker. In this situation the off-blocker (RF) must share the dink responsibility (b). When the entire front line blocks, the middle in player is in serious trouble. He must line up behind the middle blocker and rely on the end blockers to deflect balls dinked toward the side line.*

Fig. 9.22 Middle Spiker Vs. a Two-Man Block   *No. 9 delivers a quick play which traps the off-blocker at the net. The backcourt player behind No. 10 had to move closer to the net to compensate for his lack of coverage.* (Bob Van Wagner)

On a normal set, or a two-set, two blockers can reach the center spiker. Number 10 in Fig. 9.22 was held at the net by the threat of the setter (No. 9) backsetting the ball to the off-hand spiker (not shown). This trapped blocker puts extra pressure on his backcourt teammate, who must move closer to the net to compensate for his lack of court coverage.

When the end blocker joins the middle blocker to stop the center attack, the middle in player covers the area vacated by the end blocker (M1, Fig. 9.21b), rather than charging the 10-ft. line to defend against a possible "straight-down" spike angled inside the left front blocker. The right back lines up outside the middle blocker's arms to watch the attacker contact the ball. The left back lines up behind the blockers (LB, Fig. 9.21b) to field balls deflected by the block.

When all three blockers leave the floor, the three remaining defenders cannot cover the court adequately. The middle in player must cover the 300 sq. ft. of court inside the 10-ft. line, and the two remaining defenders must divide the 600 sq. ft. in the backcourt (Fig. 9.21c).

MIDDLE IN DEFENSE TO OFFENSE

The middle in defense is ideal for the transition to the three-hitter attack when a setter plays behind the block. When the best setter in the backcourt is also the best digger, the strategy may call for the setter to play in the left back where the greatest number of balls are usually hit. Normally, the middle in player will set the ball if this is the case. When there is an obvious free ball situation, the setter in the left back has ample time to run to the net before the ball is passed.

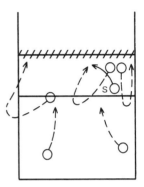

Fig. 9.23 Changing from the Middle In Defense to Offense
This can be accomplished smoothly when the setter plays behind the block.

Free balls that are passed to the left side of the court are confusing to the opponents' block and are effective if the attacking middle spiker is left-handed.

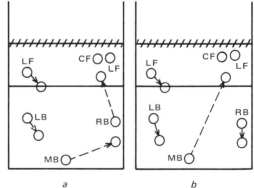

Fig. 9.24 Changing from Middle Back to Middle In Defense *This change can be initiated by a verbal command and the digger's movements on the line (RB, a) or the middle back player (MB, b).*

CHANGING DEFENSES

When a team has mastered both defenses and can play together as a cohesive unit, it is possible to change defenses in the middle of a rally. The opportune moment to change from the middle back to middle in occurs when the opposing spiker is off-balance or tires, and when the middle back or line digger expects a dink shot. A verbal signal may be exchanged prior to the switch, or it may be initiated by either backcourt player running in behind the block.

10

Coeducational and Doubles Play

COEDUCATIONAL PLAY

Playing rules for coed play are the same as those for the regulation game, with the following exceptions:

- Three males and three females per team
- Serving order alternates male, female
- When the ball is touched by more than one player on a team, one of those touches must be by a woman
- One backcourt player may also block when there is only one male player in a front line position.

Offense

Idealistically, coed play is conducted with emphasis on equal participation, a high level of sportsmanship and spirit of team play. If women are going to participate equally in coed play, they should be allowed to hit the ball over the net, even though it is 8 ft. high. Many women will not be able to spike the ball sharply down to the floor, but at least they can participate in this most exciting aspect of the game—the *spike*. For equal participation and enjoyment, the basic **M**-formation is recommended, for it allows every player to become the setter when he or she reaches the middle front position.

If the team decides that its goal is to win rather than to participate equally, it should be agreed that the male players will attempt to handle most of the blocking and spiking. When the woman is in the middle front row, the pass should be directed to the middle front and she can set the ball to either

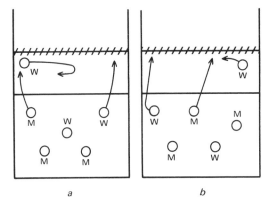

Fig. 10.1 Offense *A high ball should be passed near the center front of the court so that the setter (LF) can turn and front set the man approaching down the left side line (a). When the setter is on the right side, the ball should be passed to the right third of the court to allow the man to approach from the middle of the court and attack the ball from the on-hand side (b).*

a   *b*

Fig. 10.2 Spiking from the Center of the Court *This is a popular tactic in coed volleyball.*

end spiker. When there is only one man in the front row, he can approach from the left side if he is right-handed, and the woman on his left can switch to the center of the front court to set.

On a high pass, the woman should turn to face the man so that she can deliver a front set to him. The woman in the right front should approach for a back set. If the male spiker is a good passer, he may choose to remain in the center of the court where he can field a greater percentage of the serves. After the pass, he can spike from the center of the court.

Defense

It is possible to include two men on the block during the entire game if the woman in the middle front moves away from the net prior to the serve. In Fig. 10.3, the man in the middle back may switch with the set to the attacker's side line to enable the women to play deeper in the backcourt.

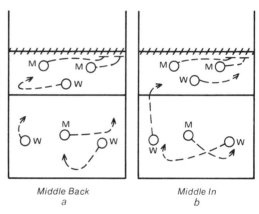

Fig. 10.3 One Woman in the Front Line   *The woman plays off-blocker position in the middle back defense (a) and the middle in position in the middle in defense (b).*

Middle Back
a

Middle In
b

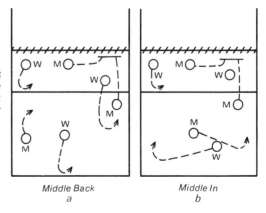

Fig. 10.4 Two Women in the Front Line   *A 1971 coed rule change allows one backcourt player to block when there is only one male player in a front line position.*

Middle Back
a

Middle In
b

When two women are in the front row, they can block the end with the man blocking the middle, or a man can be brought in from the backcourt to block. When women spikers hit on an 8-ft. net, the defense must be ready to call, "Down!" and "Free ball!"

In Fig. 10.4, the backcourt man on the side line may exchange positions with the front line women in both the middle back (a) and middle in defenses (b). In the middle in defense the remaining backcourt men and women may move toward the center of the court and switch with the set to enable the man to field the harder line spikes.

DOUBLES PLAY

Playing rules in the *Official Volleyball Guide* are the same as those for the regulation game and doubles, with the following exceptions:

- Each team's court is 30 ft. by 25 ft.
- No substitutions allowed
- Serve should come from the right half of the service area
- Game is 11 points, or 5 minutes of ball in play -- whichever occurs first

Generally, tournament directors do not use a timer, and the length of the game is increased to 15 points. When doubles are played indoors, the same light, fast regulation ball as that used in the six-man game is in play.

Offense

The server has an advantage when the "short court" rule is enforced because the serving line is 5 ft. closer to the net. This gives the receiver less time to react, and is particularly noticeable on fast, low serves directed along the server's side line. The serve should not be merely a way of putting the ball into play—it should be an offensive tactic to score points.

In doubles volleyball, most of the serving aces are scored in the short middle, on the boundary lines or in the area or "seam" that lies exactly between the two receivers. Almost all the aces scored in doubles are due to hesitation on the part of the passer. The passer may hesitate because the ball looks like it will go out of bounds, hit the net or be in his partner's receiving area. When a player is tired, the ball should be served deep in the court so the passer will have to run from the back line to the net to spike the set.

The ball should rarely be served to the poor setter because balls set over the net or deep in the setter's court are usually converted into a point for the serving team. The ball should be served repeatedly to a receiver standing in the same position only if a definite weakness has become apparent. The placement, speed, breaking action of the ball, and selection of the receiver should vary to prevent the opposition from falling into a groove.

Occasionally, the ball should be served to the stronger player, particularly if he has a tendency to relax or cover a weaker partner. When the last serve results in a serving error, the next server should take a little power off the serve to make sure it lands in fair territory.

Passing, setting and good physical endurance are the keys to attack in doubles. Almost anyone can spike well if the set is placed within a few feet of the net. Excellent spikers who do not have the necessary setting and passing skills do not enjoy great success in doubles volleyball. A poor setter must select an outstanding spiker as a partner to compensate for a lack of precision setting. Spikers must learn to vary their attack and to take advantage of the defensive player who is moving before the ball is contacted.

Many top players ask their friends for the "book" on their spiking patterns to see if they have become predictable in their attack. More successful players compete with the same player for the entire doubles season to learn where the ball will be passed and set in every situation. There is nothing more satisfying to a spiker than to know that his partner can deliver a set "right on" the net. Instead of watching the setter and trying to guess where he will place the ball, a spiker, confident in his partner's setting ability, can concentrate on a correct approach and maximum jump, which are necessary to spike well.

Pinpoint passing is not as crucial in doubles as it is in the six-man game. When the ball is passed high in the air toward the center of the court, the setter should have little difficulty in delivering a good set. The precision setting necessary to help the spiker defeat the two-man block is not absolutely necessary to successful doubles teams. A good spiker should jump high enough to spike the ball down against one blocker and one or two diggers when the ball is set within 4 ft. of the net.

Defense

Defenders find it very difficult to dig a good spiker in indoor doubles when the set is right on the net. Most of the time the poor digger should block when defending against a good set in the indoor game. If the spiker can be blocked a few times, the setter will be reluctant to put the set close to the net and the spiker may begin to "be dug" and commit spiking errors.

The most successful teams are also best on defense. Better players keep a mental "book" on their opponents and find that certain players usually hit the ball in the same place when they approach the set in a prescribed manner. The defense moves into this area before the ball is spiked and, in effect, dares the spiker to alter the attack or try a shot he does not have in his offensive arsenal.

BEACH DOUBLES

Many experts believe that the long-term national dominance of Southern California men's and women's teams stems from the mastery of basic fundamentals that are learned through long hours of practice playing beach doubles.

Official and Unwritten Rules*

Many beach doubles' rules are unwritten and vary from those published in the *Official Volleyball Guide*. The following rules and interpretations are in effect during the Southern California Beach Volleyball Tournament Schedule.

Court size is 30 ft. by 60 ft. as opposed to the 30-ft. by 50-ft. court used in indoor doubles. Instead of lines, ropes are used to block off the courts. A center rope is placed under the net only in the case of the six-man volleyball. Stepping across the center of the court below the net is legal so long as players do not interfere with the opposing team. Players may serve from anywhere behind their end line as opposed to serving from the right side of the court. The net is placed 7 ft. 10 in. above hard-packed sand, and 7 ft. 9 in. above loosely packed sand (stated in the *Guide*). Net height remains the same for mixed doubles. The vertical tape markers on the end of the net are disregarded, and the ball is considered in play if it passes between the wooden posts supporting the net.

The ball has an 18-piece leather cover and is quite heavy in comparison to the 12-panel official ball. This heavier ball is stable in the wind and is always preferred on the beach.

There are no scorers, umpires, timers or linesmen; the referee keeps score, and there are no time limits on the games. The referee usually sits on a platform attached to one of the volleyball posts. A player on the winning team in the preceding match usually referees the following match. Any player may request a time out when the ball is dead. If, in the referee's opinion, a player has too much sand on his body or in his eyes, an uncharged time out is granted.

Since no substitutions are allowed, players are also granted uncharged time outs for stretching out leg cramps. Players must keep the same serving order throughout the game, but may change court positions at any time.

Most players are left- or right-side specialists and do not change positions except during prolonged rallies. Teams change sides of the court every four points in 11-point games and every five points in 15 point games. This neutralizes the advantage of serving, setting and spiking into the wind or sun.

Blocking is permitted by any player, but is generally considered poor strategy since beach lore forbids the blocker from reaching over the net. Players who contact the net are expected to stop the play immediately and award their opponents the ball. It is considered poor form to wait for the referee to call the net foul. For that matter, it is considered a point of honor to call throws or other infractions on yourself if the referee has missed the call.

---

*For specific details regarding beach doubles' competitions and tournaments in Southern California, readers are advised to write the Santa Monica Recreation Department.

When a player participates in a block, the ball may be played only once in succession as opposed to the successive contacts allowed in USVBA rules. It is still considered "bad form" for the setter or digger to place the ball over the net before making third contact. However, if one's partner is definitely out of position, the stigma of "shooting" the ball over on the first or second contact is not frowned upon.

In mixed doubles the man is expected to hit the ball over the net after the woman contacts it. Since the net is 7 ft. 10 in., women do not generally pose much of an offensive threat.

The ball may be hit on any part of the body, including the foot, as opposed to the USVBA rule of a "dead ball" for contact below the waist. It is considered unsportsmanlike to accept a point if the referee misses the call. Protests are decided on the spot by the referee; in unique cases the tournament director will handle the protests.

Open-hand dinks are automatically "called" throws. The setter is not allowed the freedom of moving his arms across his body to deliver the set. All but the most renown setters must squarely face the direction of the intended set. Overhand passing of the serve is frowned upon and scrutinized very closely by the opposition and referee. On the other hand, overhand dig-

Fig. 10.5 Digging the Spike   *Larry Rundle prepares to overhand dig a spike by Dane Holtzman, Most Valuable Player of the 1970 NCAA Tournament. Hank Bergman moves toward the center of the court to set the dig.* (Bob Van Wagner)

Fig. 10.6 Sky Ball   *The ball is tossed a few feet in the air and contact is made with the heel of the hand. This serve is difficult to field in a high wind or if the sun is directly overhead.* (Gary Adams)

ging or passing of the spike is interpreted quite leniently, as compared to current indoor interpretations.

Beach doubles is weighted in favor of the defense because players cannot jump as high off the sand as they do off the boards and they are spiking a heavier and slower ball. The block should only be used on a perfect set, or by teams that simply cannot dig the ball adequately.

Spikers may *not* follow through over the net even though they might touch the ball on their side of the court. If the sun is directly overhead, the *sky ball serve* should be utilized. This is an underhand serve that is hit so high it looks like it is falling out of the sun. It is usually effective against players who are used to playing indoors. When the wind is blowing toward the server, the *overhand spin* serve can have an extraordinary amount of power and still stay in the opponents' court.

Part IV

ORGANIZATION

(Gary Adams)

11

Training and Conditioning

What is the secret of championship teams? How do they win year after year? The outstanding performance of teams from certain areas of the country *can* be explained.

First, the players' development must be on constant basis: year round indoor or outdoor courts must be available where young athletes have a chance to play under the guidance of experienced players and instructors.

Secondly, young players must be properly motivated to take up the sport. Tournaments must be held during all seasons to maintain constant interest. During the warmer months of the year outdoor doubles tournaments should be held in several classifications.

Third, and most important, championship teams are systematically conditioned through a well-planned seasonal training cycle.

CONDITIONING PROGRAMS

The methods of conditioning volleyball players can be separated into three groups:

- General exercises
- Increasing jumping ability
- Technique conditioning

General Exercises

Exercises without weights or the ball can develop *flexibility*, *strength* and *endurance*. *Flexibility* is particularly important in preventing muscle tears in the legs and lower back. During the blocks and spike, players are constantly contracting the muscles in their back and legs, which causes them to lose their full range of motion and thereby become subject to muscle tears and strains.

Flexibility or stretching exercises should be included in every practice session and before every match. Players should jog and perform jumping jacks to warm up their muscles before attempting stretching exercises. Slow stretching is suggested to prevent the player's muscles from tearing during warm-up. Explosive stretching exercises before the match begins will cause injuries that show up during competition.

Since muscle strains and pulls in the back and legs are relatively common volleyball injuries, it is recommended that the following exercises be included in workouts and pre-game warmups.

Stretching Exercises

Trunk Twister   Stand with feet spread shoulder-width apart and twist the body from side to side. Do not move the feet.

Alternate Toe-Toucher   Stand with feet spread more than shoulder-width apart and alternately touch toes with fingers on opposite hands.

Groin Stretcher   Spread legs considerably more than shoulder-width apart and alternately squat over one leg while fully extending the other leg.

Crossover Toe Touch   Cross legs in a fully extended standing position. Bending forward slowly from the waist, touch the ground.

Tail Gunner   Position body in a full squat. Hold toes of both feet with the fingers. Without releasing toes, slowly attempt to extend legs fully.

Quadriceps Stretch   Start from kneeling position, with hands on soles of feet. Slowly move the back of the head toward the ground.

Crossover Toe Touch   Lie flat on the back, hands outstretched at right angles to the body. Slowly raise one leg up and over the body to touch the palm of the opposite hand.

Toes over Head   Lie flat on the ground on the back and slowly raise legs up and over the head until toes touch the ground. Also, touch toes of both feet to the ground over the left and right shoulder. This is an excellent stretching exercise for preventing the lower back from tightening up.

Superior leg strength necessary for satisfactory vertical jumping height is paramount to the volleyball player. The strength of the abdominal muscles, and to a lesser degree the back muscles, also plays a large part in the player's spiking action. Experience has shown that above-average arm strength is not a prerequisite for the successful spiker. The important thing is timing, or coordination, when spiking. This is best accomplished by spiking set balls from every conceivable location and angle.

The overload theory contends that muscle cells increase in size and strength when they are taxed to the present limit of their ability to respond. Exercises of a rigorous nature are necessary when conditioning for strength.

The following exercises are recommended for workouts and, in general, are not intended as part of a pre-game warm-up.

Strength Exercises

Sit-Ups.

Jackknife Sit-Ups   Lie flat on the back. Simultaneously lift both extended legs and trunk toward each other until outstretched hands touch toes.

Power Sit-Ups   Lie flat on the back, hands clasped behind the neck and legs extended. (A partner holds the ankles.) Touch knees with elbows and return to within a foot of the floor; pause, then repeat. Do not return to the floor until the exercise is completed.

Back-Ups   Lie on the stomach, legs extended and hands clasped behind the neck. (A partner holds the ankles). Raise the upper part of the body as far off the floor as possible; return to the floor and repeat. Players with strong backs may pause a foot from the floor for a greater overload of the back muscles.

Stomach and Leg Exercise   One player lies on his back and holds ankles of his partner who stands behind him, feet shoulder-width apart. The player on the ground rapidly lifts his extended legs up over his head toward the standing player, who attempts to push the legs back toward the floor. The object of the player on the floor is to prevent his feet from returning to the ground by powerfully contracting his stomach and leg muscles.

Squats   Jump up and down two times from a full squat position; jump the third time for maximum height.

Unless a player has good *endurance*, his muscles will become tired and fail to respond properly during prolonged competition. By observing the height of a player's jump during a long match, it will become evident whether present endurance levels must be increased. An example of a good jumper with poor endurance is the spiker who contacts the ball 30 in. above the net during warm-ups and only 20 in. above the net during the fifth game. Muscular endurance is developed by repetitively working tired muscles. The athlete who has the ability to drive himself after becoming tired will gradually improve his endurance. The team that can remain physically strong throughout a five-game match or tournament can defeat technically superior teams.

Nothing hinders proper endurance faster than *overweight*. The player who is 10 pounds overweight must jump and lift that 10 pounds hundreds of times during a match. The overweight athlete must train harder than his teammates at proper weight and generally has great difficulty in maintaining proper endurance.

In recent years, overweight athletes have not been seen in international volleyball competition. Players who tend to gain weight out of season and quickly try to get back in shape during the conditioning phase of the season suffer a loss of strength, endurance and speed which puts them behind their teammates from the beginning.

Periodic weight checks throughout the year can motivate athletes to control their weight. The following endurance exercises are best utilized at the end of practice sessions.

Endurance Exercises

Sprint and Jog   Players sprint for distances of 10-30 ft., then jog on the coach's whistle. Repeat for 8–15 minutes.

Leap Frog   Groups of 6–12 players play leap frog around the gym or track for several minutes.

Elastic Jump   Zigzag a 25-ft. length of elastic to form a 6-to-18 jump obstacle course. Jump over each barrier once, then over and back and over again. Raise the height and repeat.

Rim Touch   Jump and touch a basketball rim 50 times without resting.

Net Jump   Select partners of the same height and place them on opposite sides of the net. At 5-ft. intervals the partners jump and clap their hands over the net. Repeat jump 50 times. Now jump with a double-hand clap above the net.

Step Jump   Ascend steps by jumping one or two steps at a time using a 2-ft. takeoff.

Mock Spike   Jump and simulate a spiking action using an approach and 2-ft. takeoff. Repeat 25 times in succession.

Increasing Jumping Ability

A discussion of weight-training procedures for increasing the vertical jump is necessary for players new to the team. Returning athletes who have been weight training during the post-season need to continue their program in order to maintain their increased "spring" until the end of the competitive season. The coach should provide a copy of weight-training theory and its implications for volleyball to each player.[1]

Serious players lift weights to increase the height of their vertical jump and sustain maximum jumping ability throughout long matches and tournaments. The low squatting position of backcourt players tends to sap vital leg strength and decrease the height of the jump in net play unless the legs are thoroughly conditioned. Players with a history of a bad back or injured knees should be checked by a doctor before attempting weight training.

It is recommended that untrained athletes first complete 50 consecutive squats with half of their body weight before training with heavy weights. This procedure will screen those players who are not yet safely capable of working with heavier weights.

The *theory of specificity* maintains that training is specific to the cells and to the specific structural and functional elements within a cell that are overloaded. Transfer of training occurs only to the extent that the same muscle fibers are recruited and used in a similar manner.[2]

When weight training to increase vertical jumping height during the spike, the player should squat just as low as he would in competition. Slow-motion films may be utilized to determine knee angle and lateral foot spacing.

If the spiker is using the correct technique, his feet should be almost parallel. He should extend his legs as quickly as possible so that the muscle fibers are used as they are in competition. Players with strong backs and arms may add a further refinement by jumping with a barbell held behind their neck above the shoulders. The jump should be made as quickly as possible, and the arms should push against the barbell to prevent the neck from supporting its weight. The back should be kept straight to prevent strain or tear when the athlete lands on the floor. The shock of returning to the floor must be absorbed by a controlled squatting action to prevent damage to the supportive structure surrounding the knee joints and vertebrae.

The *theory of strength training* contends that lifting weights from one to six times with maximum effort is the most effective method of producing skeletal muscle hypertrophy (size) and increasing muscle strength. This training should be carried out through the full range of motion required in the athlete's skill.[3] Training to increase the height of the vertical jump may be done every other day, however; "Many athletics will experience an additional gain of five to ten percent in vertical jumping height by daily lifts."[4]

The *theory of overload* contends that for skeletal muscle cells to increase in size or functional ability or both they must be taxed to the limit of their present ability to respond.[5] (Italics added)

As additional strength is gained, more weight can be added to the program to insure continued gains. Increasing the weight gradually is mandatory for preventing excessive stretching of ligamental tissue surrounding the joint. When the muscles become fatigued or weight is excessive, full weight is placed on the ligaments.[6]

"*Rapid movements* should result in the selective recruitment of the faster fibers."[7] (Italics added) Speed training requires the movement of light loads at a high velocity compatible with correct technique. When training for leg speed it is suggested that a light weight be used in three sets of ten explosive jumping squats.

The *theory of endurance training* maintains that the "interaction of load, speed, and duration may be successfully resolved by either continuous exercise or intermittent exercise".[8] The important point is to overload the muscle group or groups.

Experience has shown that 50 daily, full-controlled squats with 50 percent of a player's body weight builds the leg endurance necessary to maintain the low defensive backcourt position throughout a long tournament.

Weight-Training Program

1. To gain additional jumping height, squat one to six times with the maximum amount of weight that is capable of being lifted in good form. Add weight to the program as quickly as the muscles can safely handle the additional load.

2. To build and maintain the ability to stay in a low defensive position, perform 50 consecutive full-controlled squats with 50 percent body weight.

3. To develop speed, strength and endurance, perform three sets of ten explosive jumping squats with the maximum amount of weight that can be safely handled for 30 repetitions.

Some players prefer to lift daily; there seems to be a slight gain in strength for most individuals when following a daily program as opposed to lifting on alternate days.

Technique Conditioning

Working tired muscles through rigorous drills of any type leads to greater muscular endurance. Experience has shown that the following drills are particularly suited to condition players as they practice techniques.

Jump Set   Three setters stand 10 ft. apart in a straight line along the net and, taking a maximum jump, set the ball to one another. The setter in the middle jumps and back sets the ball.

Endurance Spike   The spiker hits 40 sets in a row as quickly as possible. The rest of the players retrieve the balls to insure continuous action.

Endurance Blocking   One blocker moves across the net and blocks the left, middle and right spikers in rotation. The setter delivers a ball to the next spiker as the blocker completes the jump. Ten to fifteen trips across the front row blocking all three positions are usually sufficient.

Running Dig   The player starts on the side line and runs toward the middle of the back line to dig a spike hit from the net. After diving or rolling to dig the ball, the player returns to the original starting position and repeats the action.

Backcourt Defense   If using the middle in defense, station a player in each deep corner of the backcourt and a middle in player in the center of the court on the 10-ft. line. Two spikers stand on tables in the left and right spiking positions and maintain a continuous attack directed at the three defenders who attempt to dig and set the ball to targets in the front corners of their court. The rest of the players retrieve balls to insure no break in the action.

Diving Save   The coach stands on a table and dinks balls over the net to a player in a backcourt defensive position. The player runs and makes a diving pass to a target and returns to the starting position. The drill should then be repeated.

Block Rebounds The player squats 3 ft. from a flat wall and reacts to spikes rebounding off the wall. The spiker stands a few feet behind the player and delivers an assortment of hard and off-speed spikes and dinks against the wall for the player to dig. The player fielding the simulated block rebound should squat in a 90-degree–115-degree angle to pass the ball straight up in the air.

Backcourt Spiking Game Two or three players form a team and play a regulation game with one exception: The ball cannot be spiked unless the player leaves the floor from behind the 10-ft. spiking line. This game is particularly effective at the end of a long practice when extra motivation is desirable to work tired muscles.

SEASONAL TRAINING CYCLE

The USVBA defines the volleyball season as "the period from November 1 of one calendar year to June 1 of the next calendar year."[9] Due to vacations, it is usually very difficult to get teams together to practice before October 1—particularly if it is a school or college team.

Although tournaments begin in November in certain parts of the country, the important tournaments and league matches usually do not get under way until late February. Therefore, it is recommended that a conditioning program commence in October and continue until the holiday period in December.

The team might meet as a group on Tuesdays and Thursdays and work on individual conditioning programs on Monday, Wednesday and Friday. The coach should schedule a conference with each player and develop an individualized program that takes into account the age, physical condition, experience and present skill level of each athlete so that the player will have a personalized plan of improvement.

The attitude of the players during this individual conference cannot be overlooked. Players must want to develop strength, endurance, flexibility and speed, and to learn the basic theories of conditioning to train effectively. Explanations of the cardiovascular and respiratory systems and principles of strength, endurance, flexibility and speed training are invaluable to the athlete.

Conditioning Phase

During group workouts the team should concentrate on strength and flexibility exercises as well as technical training on the approach and jump for the spike. Technical mastery of the dive and roll also should be stressed. During the second half of the two- or three-hour practice, individual and partner ball handling skills utilized in the pass, set, dig, dive and roll should be stressed. These drills should be as rigorous as possible so that the players may build up endurance in the muscle groups to be used in competition.

To be effective, the conditioning should be gradual and repetitive. To insure continuous improvement the intensity and duration should correspond to the strength and ability of the team members. The striving for maximum conditioning within a short period is rarely possible and may cause injury to the athlete.

After some of the prospective players are cut from the squad, the second hour should also include individual technical training in the block, spike and serve. The final squad cut to 12 players can be made at the last practice before the Christmas holidays. Some teams may choose to carry about 18 players on the squad and enter two teams in tournament competition to give the younger players valuable experience.

During the conditioning program the players must learn the physiological principles that contribute to effective power and endurance development and the proper methods of power and endurance training. Conditioning will not be successful if it is merely thought of as repeated physical exercise. Coaches must explain the reasons for a particular exercise or drill and how it relates to achieving success in the sport. It is important that players understand the techniques and tactics for which they are developing their capabilities.

Experience has shown that when players acquire the practical and theoretical knowledge of volleyball while developing physical qualities, the morale and will power necessary to build and maintain a high level of conditioning are enhanced.

Seasonal Training Cycle

Month	Training Phase	Physical Training %	Technical Training %	Tactical Training %
Oct.	Conditioning	70	25	5
Nov.	Conditioning	70	25	5
Dec.	Conditioning	65	25	10
Jan.	Preparatory	35	40	25
Feb.	Competitive	35	35	30
Mar.	Competitive	30	35	35
Apr.	Special training cycle for playoffs			

Some volleyball teams win tournaments at the beginning of the season, but achievements decline toward the height of the season. If this is the case, research might prove that the athletes had a great deal of weight training and running at the beginning of the season but had ignored this training phase during the preparatory and competitive stages. For some time the level of the athlete's strength and endurance may remain high; therefore, the results will also be high. Gradually, however, in view of the absence of exercise for strength development, strength will decrease and so will performance.

Preparatory Phase

During the preparatory phase, the volleyball is used in physical training. At this stage the athlete develops through technical training in spiking, blocking and digging. The coach might stand on a ladder and spike balls just out of the player's effective range of movement. The digger reacts to the spiked ball by running and diving or rolling to retrieve the spike, coming to his feet, and digging the next spike, and so on. When the digger is exhausted, he retrieves balls for the coach while a fresh player takes his place.

On the other court a player may be spiking 30 or 40 consecutive sets while his teammates quickly retrieve the balls to insure continuous action. A blocking drill can be formed for building endurance by aligning one blocker against three spikers. As the player completes the block, the next spiker passes the ball and approaches for the set. The blocker must move as quickly as possible from one spiker to another.

It is important that every player participate during these drills, either running balls down or feeding balls to the coach. Players develop a sense of pride by performing as well as possible during the drills and "gutting it out" until their turn ends. Teammates who endure the same conditioning procedure should yell encouragement and try to motivate the occasional goldbricker to perform up to his utmost physical capabilities. The coach should continually alert his players to use correct technique during these endurance drills to prevent bad habits from being formed.

The preparatory phase of the season may last from four to six weeks. Although practice matches and tournaments may play an important role in the motivation of the athlete during this phase, the emphasis during practice should be on technical execution and conditioning with team tactics of attack and defense being refined in competition.

Preparatory Training Cycle

Week	Main Purpose	Intensity of Work
1	Development of technique	Medium
2	Improvement of technique	Heavy
3	Development of strength and endurance	Maximum
4	Blending of technique and tactics	Medium
5	Improvement of tactics	Medium to light

During practice matches, many different player combinations and rotations should be used and evaluated subjectively by the coaches and statistically by trained managers who chart serves, passes, sets, spikes, blocks and digs. Coaches use competition in the preparatory phase for purposes of evaluating starting line-ups and seeing which substitutes react well in pressure situations.

The coaching staff should still stress the *what* and *why* of every drill so that the team understands clearly and precisely the problems involved in training. Some players may choose to drop weight training to twice a week, while other players may prefer to continue daily weight training.

Competitive Phase

The competitive phase begins when standings are kept for league play or selection to regional and national tournaments. For the first time during the season the team members should know who is in the starting line-up and who they will be playing next to on offense. Up to one-third of the practice should be devoted to team tactics, with emphasis on team passing, blocking and digging.

Individual and team weak points in competition should be worked on in practice. Players should be shown the charts and statistics on their performances, and drills should be developed to minimize their errors. Drills and scrimmages will vary according to the imperfections discovered in the last match or tournament. The finer points of team tactics such as backing up the block and switching from offense to defense should be stressed.

Physical conditioning should not be isolated from fundamental techniques and playing tactics during the competitive phase. Physical, technical and tactical training must be developed concurrently for best results. Depending on the stage of the season and the progress of the individuals and team, time should be allotted to specific areas of training. The coach must be flexible enough to adjust practice schedules to the progress of the team's development.

During the competitive phase the substitutes should become *specialists*. Often a single player may fill many specialized roles. Specialists with the following capabilities are needed:

- A player who can serve for points in crucial situations
- A substitute with the ability to "fire the team up" or make them perform beyond expectation
- A journeyman setter with good ball handling skills
- A utility spiker who is a good all-around performer
- An excellent passer and backcourt defensive specialist
- A good hitter and blocker to substitute across the front row

Specialists should not be selected until it becomes obvious that they will not earn a starting position. For example, if a player is too small to spike effectively and cannot handle the ball well enough to set, he can still contribute to his team's success by perfecting his serve, pass and backcourt defensive skills.

Substitutes should know the situations that they might be required to play, and should receive extra practice in their specialties during the competitive phase of the season. This differs from the preparatory phase when all players participate in the same drills.

During the competitive stage of the season, it is important that maximum workouts do not occur the day before the match or tournament. Maximum practice sessions should occur twice a week if a match or tournament is scheduled; three times a week if there is no contest during that week.

Special Phases

Before a championship tournament, it is often helpful to simulate practice sessions in the same cycle that will occur in the forthcoming competition. Let us assume that to win a championship a team must play three matches on Friday and two matches on Saturday. Since most teams are used to a light workout on Friday and a heavy tournament schedule on Saturday, they may have difficulty in playing at a high level on both days unless prior training is distributed in the same intensity as the championship event.

The coach must constantly be on guard against players "going stale" because practices are too frequent and prolonged. If this situation occurs, he should vary the drills when planning practice sessions at the conclusion of a long season so the players will be mentally ready for the important matches or tournaments. Scheduled practices may need to be cancelled in instances where inadequate rest or mental fatigue take hold.

Schools and college teams often find that they have lost their momentum after a final exam period because practices were held on a volunteer basis for those student athletes who could spare the time from their studies. During the first week after exams, the coach must decide whether to take a long- or short-range view in planning practices. Should he attempt to regain his players' technical skills through rigorous practice on the fundamentals or stress offensive and defensive tactics for the next opponent? It is best to take the long-range view and emphasize technique if the team has a good chance of qualifying for the playoffs.

WEEKLY AND DAILY SCHEDULE

It is best to outline the weekly practice sessions in advance and develop the daily sessions in detail at the conclusion of each practice.

Weekly Schedule

Workouts that are scheduled for maximum intensity should be followed with practices of less intensity. As a general rule, only two all-out workouts should be scheduled during a competition week. If no competition is scheduled, three maximum workouts during a five-day a week practice schedule are often appropriate. The athlete should recuperate sufficiently from previous heavy exercise before the next heavy conditioning session. Several heavy conditioning sessions in a row usually are not effective and may be harmful to the athlete's health.

Repeated drills are necessary for the formation of a conditioned reaction. For example, if a player has to think about diving to dig a spike, he will move too late to reach the ball. When the same player has dived to retrieve balls thousands of times in practice he will automatically dive for a ball in competition. There is little development or improvement without repetitive conditioning. It is the coach's responsibility to develop varied drills that repetitively develop the same technique.

Daily Practice

A practice session can consist of four parts.

Part 1   Warm-up and stretching exercises, partner ball handling skills
Part 2   Technique drills which cover the pass, set, spike, block and dig
Part 3   Team drills for mastering tactics
Part 4   Scrimmages and endurance drills

Practice Outline—Preparatory Phase

1. Warm-Up (30 min.)
   Laps and exercises
   Partner drills—emphasis on passing and setting
   Pepper
2. Technique (80 min.)
   Drills to correct individual weaknesses
   Setting and attacking
   Blocking
   Digging
   Individual serving and receiving
3. Tactics (40 min.)
   Offense
   Defense
4. Scrimmage and conditioning (20–40 min.)
   Scrimmaging
   Endurance drills

While experienced coaches may prefer to work from a simple outline, others may choose a more detailed practice plan. These plans should be evaluated and dated for the coach's reference throughout the season. Whole sections may be omitted from certain practices, particularly in the competitive phase when practice sessions should be used to strengthen weak points that show up in competition.

Detailed Practice Outline—Preparatory Phase

1. Warm-up (30 min.)
   Laps and exercises
   Touch block

    Mock block
    Dives
    Rolls
    Pepper

2. Technique drills (80 min.)
    Attack and setting
        Left
        Right
        Dinks--L, M, R
        Deep sets--L, R
        4's
        3's
        1's
        Middle 2's
        Right 2's
        Right x
        1-2
        High middle
    Blocking
        3 vs. 3
        2 vs. 3
    Digging
    Serving and receiving
        Front court
        Back court
        Team
        Pass and hit--1's
    Individual skills
        Defense
        Blockers
        Setters

3. Tactics (40 min.)
    Offense
    Defense
    Game preparation
        Back-up spiker
        Free ball
        Down block
        Special

4. Scrimmage and conditioning (20-40 min.)
    Offense and defense scrimmage
    Spike
    Block
    Dig
    Special conditioning

REFERENCES

1. Faulkner, John A. New perspectives in training for maximum performance. *The Journal of the American Medical Association*, 205, 11 (Sept. 9, 1968), pp. 117-122.

2. Ibid., p. 119.

3. Ibid., p. 119.

4. Major, David. (Pan American Weightlifting Coach). 29 July 1967, personal interview with the author.

5. Faulkner. New perspectives in training for maximum performance. See p. 117.

6. Bender, Jay A. Some guidelines for the development of exercise programs. *The Physical Educator* (May 1966), pp. 60-62.

7. Faulkner. New perspectives in training for maximum performance. See p. 119.

8. Faulkner. New perspectives in training for maximum performance. See p. 120.

9. Shondell, Donald S. (Ed.) *1971 Official rules and reference guide.* Berne, Ind.: United States Volleyball Association. See p. 18.

12

Responsibilities of the Coach

PHILOSOPHY

The coach's philosophy is usually determined by self-image and his analysis of what constitutes a successful season.

The *idealist* is interested in developing the team's best potential. In attempting to achieve excellence, he stresses teamwork and wants each player to maintain his own individuality. Sportsmanship and honor on and off the court are goals of the idealistic coach also. He feels that every possible opportunity should be given to players with poorer skills to develop their fundamental techniques. Consequently, there will not be a "starting six" until the lesser-skilled players are convinced that they were selected only after everyone had an equal chance to display his talents.

The idealistic coach will divide his attention among all the players and give substitutes a reasonable chance to try new positions. The poor passer, setter, spiker, server or digger will be allowed to play his position and not be covered or substituted out of the game. He will give every player opportunities to improve weaker skills during game competition, thus building confidence and helping members become all-around players.

The *realist* is likely to develop a starting line-up early in the season and concentrate on "starters" during practice sessions. Starting players are usually run through a rigorous conditioning program. Substitutes will be carried on the team as long as they maintain the desire to improve themselves. When they complain about their lack of playing time, they might be told that they should feel free to leave the squad. The realistic coach generally finishes the season with a smaller squad than the idealist.

The realist chooses an offense and defense suited to the abilities of the best players. He is not concerned with developing all-around players and relies on the best talents of each player to develop a winning team.

Poor passers will find themselves under the net when they are in the front row and on the end line when they are in the back row. Poor diggers may find themselves playing the middle in position behind the blockers during their three rotations across the back row. Setters in the two-hitter attack might not be set unless there is an emergency, because their practice time has been devoted to setting. Setters in the three-hitter attack, who are less capable spikers than their teammates, may be directed to approach for the one-set in the middle from two spiking positions as decoys to hold the middle blocker. Spikers who have not had adequate setting practice may be pushed out of the way by aggressive setters when they have stepped in to set an errant pass. Poor servers and passers may be removed from the backcourt until their skills are perfected in practice sessions.

The *pragmatist* may start the game by using an offense and defense which provide equal participation. If this tactic proves successful, he will maintain this strategy throughout the season. If the team starts to falter during competition, each player will become specialized in a particular role.

The *existentialist* might have all the players participate in every fundamental aspect of the game. When each player finds out how he can contribute to the success of his team, he will then be expected to accept the roles of his teammates.

Most coaches develop a unique philosophy that is a blend of the philosophies listed above and cannot be easily classified.

PRACTICE SESSIONS

Coach and team must decide upon their goals and aspirations for the coming season. If a team is formed for the recreational value of the sport, it can probably compete well enough to enjoy itself in a low level of competition with one practice a week. The team that aspires to become the national champion must practice longer and harder than the opposition, unless they are substantially physically, technically and tactically superior to the competition.

Although most volleyball championships are conducted in late April or early May, some teams begin practicing as early as October. College teams that conduct fall practice usually meet as a group on Tuesdays and Thursdays, with the players lifting weights and running at their own convenience on Monday, Wednesday and Friday.

The best example of an all-out practice schedule that was undertaken by amateurs who had to maintain regular working hours was provided in 1964 by the Japanese Women Olympic Volleyball Champions. In Japan, each Olympic team works together at the same business company. This particular team worked at a company called Nichibo, along with Coach Hirobumi Daimatsu.

They kept strict office hours from 8:00 A.M. to 4:30 P.M. and practiced only after the completion of the working day. Since their strongest competition was expected to come from a professional Russian women's team, Coach Daimatsu devised the most rigorous training schedule ever attempted by a group of amateur athletes:

Nichibo Girls' Daily Schedule

8:00 A.M.	Workday begins
4:30 P.M.	Workday ends
5:00 P.M.	Training starts
6:30 P.M.	Snack
6:40 P.M.	Training resumes
11:00 P.M.	Training ends
1:00 or 2:00	Sleep

WE WILL DO WHAT IS IMPOSSIBLE:

We endured the hard training and five hours sleep, to win the World Volleyball Championship. When I considered their play insufficient, I made them try over and over again, however late it might be, until they could play sufficiently and completely—that was *my way* of training, though the severity of our training often made by-standers shut their eyes. I cried, "Do you think that you can defeat the Russian team in such a clumsy manner!!!" Many times we practiced until the eastern sky became bright. It was getting late, they could not do what I asked them to do—Even their Captain, Miss Kasai, sometimes protested against me. "Coach! Do you think we can do such a thing?" If I had given into her and softened the hardness of training, all our suffering up to that time, would have come to nothing. I rejected her protest. *"Do what is impossible."*

Orientation

An *orientation meeting* for all prospective players should be scheduled prior to the first day of practice. This meeting is necessary for setting the standards for the season; it should begin precisely at the prescribed time and be planned as carefully as any practice session. The following material can be covered in 90 minutes:

- Completion of player questionnaire*
- Discussion of team standards
- Eligibility rules
- Playing rules and rule changes
- Weight training
- Presentation of basic offense

---

* See Appendix, page 254.

- Evaluation of previous season and expectations of forthcoming season
- Season practice and competitive schedule
- Physical examination
- Locker room procedure
- Reporting for first practice

A clear understanding of team standards is important. The coach must not back himself into a corner by setting standards that are unrealistic for the team to live up to. A growing number of athletes resent a coach who places regulations on their grooming habits. If long hair interferes with performance, the coach is responsible for pointing out this flaw; and, the team members must correct them. Team members must also remember that only the coach is authorized to decide on who will play.

Complete understanding of eligibility rules for all the competition planned for the upcoming season is imperative. For colleges, this means school, conference and association eligibility requirements. All technical eligibility questions should be referred to the regular institutional eligibility authority.

Playing rules and rule changes and their implications should be discussed at the orientation meeting as well as at selected practices throughout the season. More than one match has been lost in national competition because of illegal substitutions and other rule infractions, simply because the team was not aware of current rules.

A film demonstrating the basic fundamentals of the serve, pass, set, spike, dive and role is valuable.[+] If the film is not in slow motion, a projector with reverse and stop action should be utilized to reinforce critical teaching points.

The performance of last year's team should be evaluated and related to expectations of the upcoming season. The coach should give this analysis considerable thought, for it can provide the proper motivation for the extensive physical conditioning during the early season workouts.

The preparatory and competitive stages of training should be outlined, and the players should understand the emphasis the coach will be placing on physical, technical and tactical training as the season progresses. Season practice, tournament and match schedules should be made available to each player.

No player should be allowed to practice until he has had a physical examination. It is recommended that the coach reserve a block of time for physicals and follow through with a *no physical-no practice* rule.

The last items on the agenda should be locker room and equipment procedure and instructions for reporting to the first practice.

[+] See page 249.

SCOUTING AND STATISTICS

The utilization of charts and statistics contributes to the scouting of team and individual strengths and weaknesses. In the beginning of the season, experience has shown that it is far more valuable to have your own team scouted by assistant coaches, managers or substitutes than to compile information on opposing teams.

Team Error Charts are particularly valuable in helping determine the amount of time one should allocate to the various fundamentals during practice sessions. Errors committed while serving, passing and setting should be charged to players who mishandle or misdirect the ball. Spiking errors include fouling, hitting out of bounds or into the net and being blocked for a point or side out.

Because of the amount of subjective judgment necessary to determine whether a spiked ball should have been blocked or allowed to pass over the net, blocking errors are recorded only when the player touches the net or steps over the center line while attempting to block. A position error is charged when the opposition scores a point or side out because of poor court position. The better teams force their opponents to commit errors by serving accurately, blocking well and keeping the ball in play.

Team Error Chart*

Game	Serve	Pass	Set	Spike	Block	Position	Total Errors	Score
I	2	1	6	5	0	0	14	⑮-12
II	2	3	1	8	1	2	17	⑭-16
III	1	1	3	9	0	0	14	⑮-9
IV	1	4	3	10	0	1	19	⑦-15
V	1	4	2	6	3	3	19	⑪-15
Match Totals	7	13	15	38	4	6	83	62-67

*The score of the team being charted is circled.

Good physical endurance prevents increased errors during the crucial fifth game of a match. Blocking and positioning errors usually mount up during this period because tired players begin to foul on the block and fail to maneuver into proper court position. Teams that average errors on more than two blocks, two serves, three passes, three sets or eight spikes a game should devote more practice time to developing these fundamental skills. In varsity competition, seventeen errors per game is usually the turning point between victory and defeat.

Until fundamental skills are satisfactorily developed, the most clever systems of offense and defense will not be executed correctly.

HOME TEAM RECEIVING CHART

Date __4/15__ Home Team _____ Score __15, 12, 15, 13, 15__ Rater __De Fonseca__

Visitors _____ Score __7, 15, 5, 15, 10__ Game __1–5__

Serving Order / Player and Number	6-0 Offense +	6-0 Offense 0	6-0 Offense −	4-Man Receive +	4-Man Receive 0	4-Man Receive −	4-2 Offense +	4-2 Offense 0	−
1. Kilgour	44 / 1 ④ / 3	22 / 3 ③	22 / 3 / ③	111 / 2 ④	1111 / 2 ⑤	1 / ①	22222 / ⑤	2 / ①	—
sub Shirley						11 / ②			
2. Holtzman	4 5 / 3 2 ④			22 / 5 ③			333 / ③	3333 / ④	
sub									
3. Irvin	5 / 1	44 / ④	11 / 44 ④	4 / ①	222 / ③	2 / 111 ④	1 / 2 ②		
sub Zajec	5 / 3 ②	4 / 1 ②	1 / ①		2 / ①	2 / ①			
4. Becker	222222 / 1111 ⑩	22222 / 555 ⑭	22222 / 11 ⑩		33 / 1 ③				
sub		22 / 1111	222						
5. Machado		33 / ②	3 / ①						
sub Welch						2 / ①			
6. Herring	222 1 / 44 ⑦ 3	111 / 2 ④	2222 / 33 ⑥				111 / ③		
sub									
Totals	31	29	25	7	13	7	11	5	—

+ A pass that can be set into a perfect one-play
0 A pass that can be set to either end spiker
− An ace or pass that can be set only to one spiker or a pass that must be set by a spiker

Record the area of the court the passer was in

Net _____

```
3    4    5
   2    1
```

Net _____

```
       4
          5
3            6
   2      1
```

Net _____

```
4              5
          2
   3           1
```

Individual Error Chart for Starting Players

Player	Games Played	Errors	Average Errors
A	$4\frac{1}{2}$	7	1.6
B	5	6	1.2
C	5	15	3
D	4	18	4.5
E	5	15	3
F	4	4	1

An Individual Error Chart can aid in the selection of a starting line-up. An average player will commit approximately three errors per game.

According to the Individual Error Chart, players A, B and F played an outstanding match, averaging under two errors per game. Player D committed eighteen errors in four games.

Individual Error Chart for Substitute Players

Player	Games Played	Errors	Average Errors
G	$\frac{1}{2}$	2	4
H	$\frac{1}{2}$	2	4
I	$\frac{1}{2}$	3	6
J	1	6	6
K			
L			

If a player makes an outstanding number of errors, a separate chart should be maintained on his performance, incorporating the same headings as shown in the Team Error Chart. The findings should clearly focus on the player's specific areas of weakness, and upon seeing his record he should be motivated to improve his basic skills.

A simple serve-receiving chart evaluating each player's passes should be kept on *both* teams. The serve-receiving chart (Home Team Receiving Chart) is a compilation of a five-game match. The home team received 85 serves in a 6-0 offensive formation which was used in four of six rotations. During the course of the match, the players passed 27 serves in their four-man receiving pattern. This indicates receiving trouble in that rotation. The four-two offense or two-hitter attack was used in one rotation. They only received 16 serves, and the offense was quite successful.

With this information the next practice session should have been devoted to improving the team passing and attack in the four-man receiving pattern, with particular attention given to the passing of Kilgour, Irvin and Becker.

OPPONENT PASSING CHART

Date __4/15__   Visitors _____   Score __7, 15, 5, 15, 10__   Rater __Doplemore__
                Home _____   Score __15, 12, 15, 13, 15__   Game __1–5__

Serving Order / Player and Number	6-0 Offense			4-Man Receive			4-2 Offense		
	+	0	−	+	0	−	+	0	−
1. Floyd	4	11	22 141	1222	3 11	111111 11111 22			
sub Payne	352	22 115	1111 22 223		1	33			
2. Skalecki						333			
sub Stevenson			25		6				
3. Marlowe	1 22	2		2	1	1111			
sub									
4. McFarland	4	21	111122	11222	1122	22222 111 3			
sub Zuelich									
5. Cantor	1 222	1 2222 3 5	2222 22222 346	3	111 3	1112 33			
sub									
6. Carey	11 22	22	1 2 55	122	222	1222			
sub									
Totals	16	19	38	14	16	42			

+ A pass that can be set into a perfect one-play
0 A pass that can be set to either end spiker
− An ace or pass that can be set only to one spiker or a pass that must be set by a spiker

Record the area of the court the passer was in

Net _____   Net _____   Net _____

3   4   5   4   4   5
  2   1   5   2
                  3   6   3   1
                2   1

The uncircled numbers represent the area of the court in which the player received the serve (see the key at the bottom of the chart). The circled numbers represent the total number of serves received in that column.

During that same match the home team manager charted the passing of the opponents. This chart helped the home team coach decide where the ball should be served during every rotation. For example, Floyd (see Opponent Passing Chart) passed five balls from the left back when his team was in a four-man receiving pattern; three passes were perfect and two could only be set well to one spiker. When he was in the right back, he only made one perfect pass out of fourteen attempts and thus was selected as a future serving target the next time the two teams met.

After rating the opposition for a few matches, it should become apparent where serves should be directed. Secondary targets should also be selected in the event the opposition covers the court for the target or removes the poor passer from the game.

Observe the opponents' outstanding spiker or team leader and note his passing weaknesses. An effective tactic which often pays big dividends is to serve the star player consistently, in the hope that the continuing pressure will cause him to err and destroy the team's confidence in him. Some players cannot take pressure and should be served when they begin to cover less court position as the game nears completion.

The most effective spiker on any team can be identified through the formula

$$E = \frac{U-M}{A}$$

E   efficiency
U   returnable balls which the spiker has attacked for a point or side out
M   errors—balls blocked for a point or side out; balls hit into the net or out of bounds
A   attempts—number of balls set to the spiker; balls that the spiker hits or dinks; balls returned by opponents

The Attack Chart can be used during the match for purposes of setting strategy or for substituting spikers. This chart is the compilation of a five-game match. By analyzing the attack from the left side first, we can see that Kilgour received the most sets although he barely had a plus spiking percentage. The opposition had aligned its best blockers against him and the setters should have been instructed to use him as a decoy and set another spiker opposed by weaker blockers. Although Herring had an excellent percentage from the right side, it is apparent, from his minus average, that he needed a lot of practice on the left.

The team's middle attack went well, with the exception of Irvin and Zajec. Both of these men needed much practice on the one-play which was synonomous to the middle attack.

It is important to find a solution to poor spiking efficiency. In Irvin's case the setter had to give him greater opportunity to attack from the middle

ATTACK CHART

Date __4/15__   Home Team   Score __15, 12, 15, 13, 15__   Rater __Pelton__
Game No. __1-5__   Visitors   Score __7, 15, 5, 15, 10__   Event __Match__

Serving Order	Left			Middle			Right		
Player and Number	+	0	−	+	0	−	+	0	−
1. Machado	3	2	1	3		1	1		
sub									
2. Becker	7	2	2	8		1	10	4	1
sub									
3. Irvin	3	3	1			2	5	2	3
sub Zajec	2	2	1	1	2				3
4. Kilgour	5	4	4	6	5	2	10	1	
sub									
5. Holtzman	6	2	3	4		1	6		
sub									
6. Herring	4	1	5	3		2	8	2	2
sub									
Totals	30	16	17	24	6	11	40	9	9

+ Balls resulting in a point or side out
0 Attempt that does not result in score by either team
− Error, stuff, foul, spike or dink which allows the other team to score

Spiking efficiency $= \dfrac{U - M}{A}$

E Efficiency   *U* Un-Returnable balls   *M* Mistakes
A Attempts

position in competition. If the spiker and setter could not perfect the one-play in that rotation, Irvin could not hold the middle blocker and the opposition could mount a two-man block on the end spikers. Zajec still had difficulty coming off the bench to substitute and had to stay warm during the game to regain the effectiveness he had displayed as a starter. Kilgour, Herring, Holtzman and Becker were almost unstoppable from the right.

Analyzing Attack by Spiking Position

Player	Composite	Left	Middle	Right
Kilgour	319/.250	214	356	250
Lee	165/.230	294	250	090
Holtzman	123/.203	044	304	203
Toyoda	170/.200	180	146	200
Madison	200/.180	279	065	180
Herring	208/.178	163	040	178

Before a league match begins, it is well to complete the spiking statistics of the six leading spikers against four or five of the toughest teams that have been faced. The Analyzing Attack by Spiking Position chart represents the spiking statistics of a college team against teams that finished the season as the top four finishers in the USVBA National Championships. Statistics are not meaningful when compiled against weak competition.

After reviewing the statistics, the players are put in their game line-ups and the setter delivers balls to them in their weakest position against the best available blockers while the coaching staff evaluates their techniques and spiking tactics.

In Holtzman's case, he was not receiving enough sets on the left side because the setter had lost confidence in his spiking ability. By keeping a spiking diagram with arrows drawn on a scale court it was determined that better opponents were continually giving him the line shot on his power side and taking advantage of his habit of hitting cross court spikes. He worked hard on developing his line shot and finished the season with a .312 percentage on the left side.

Madison and Herring devoted themselves to mastering the one-play in the middle and brought their meager averages up to .307 and .333 respectively, in that position by the end of the season.

By analyzing the attack, it was found that the setters had fallen into a predictable pattern of delivering the set to Kilgour when they were playing against strong competition. His early effectiveness had made this tactic acceptable, but the team attack had become too predictable. The danger of continually going to the power spiker catches up to a team when he has an off-day or when the opponent aligns its two best blockers against the star spiker. Then, the setters must deliver the ball to those players who have been relatively ignored during the competition.

It is best to move the sets around to keep the attack unpredictable and give all three attackers the motivation to approach for every spike with the anticipation of receiving the set.

As the season progresses into the competitive stage, more practice time is usually devoted to the finer points of team tactics at the expense of conditioning. It is particularly important at this stage to chart the spikers' performance by game to ascertain their endurance at the end of a long match. The Spiker Efficiency by Game chart identifies a tired spiker who should have been substituted out of the fifth game.

Spiker Efficiency by Game

Game	Unreturn-able Balls	Mis-takes	Balls Re-turned	Total Attempts	Game Average
1	5	2	1	8	.375
2	6	2	-	8	.500
3	5	1	3	9	.444
4	4	1	-	5	.600
5	5	3	2	10	.200
Match Totals	25	9	6	40	.400

An Offensive Scouting Report (see rotations opposite) can be compiled from passing and spiking charts of the opposition. This report should be discussed with the team during the practice before and immediately prior to the match so that they will understand why defenses are being altered and why serves should be directed at particular areas of the court.

An explanation by the coach must accompany the brief notes on the charts if the game strategy is to be meaningful. The strategy for the scouting report in the Offensive Scouting Report could be presented in the manner presented here on the night before the match.

In Rotation 1, the best place to serve is to B's right, close to the net. B is their best spiker and receives significantly more sets than any other player. Although he is a good passer, he has trouble recovering to spike when he is pulled to his right and close to the net to receive the serve. It is to their advantage to start in this rotation because of B's spiking ability, and we assume they will start there tomorrow night. Therefore, Kilgour will serve to the opponent in this rotation, and will practice serving to the three areas indicated in the chart.

C has rarely received a serve when he is in the right front position and has not passed well from here. If B gets in a groove, we will serve to their right front. Be sure to serve very short or he'll let the ball go to L, who is an excellent passer. R has trouble in the left back when he has to receive balls over B's right shoulder or O's left shoulder. He is an excellent passer if the ball is served directly at him. Becker will block the middle and Herring will block the line against B.

Since B hits very high and deep into our court, we'll attempt to soft block and deflect the ball to our backcourt diggers. Herring can come off the line more than usual since B doesn't go inside the end blocker but prefers to hit over the block. We'll use the middle in defense, with Kilgour playing behind our end blocker when B spikes. Do not play outside the end blocker until B hits the line. Irvin will play middle in although B will not dink unless he is in trouble. We expect Becker to deflect spikes to your area. Do not attempt to field the hard spike or you'll cut off Holtzman in the right back. Holtzman should get most of B's spikes. Start deeper than usual, as most of his spikes hit a few feet from the back line. He hits with a lot of topspin and rarely hits out. The off-blocker will be Machado. When the set goes to B, get as far off the net

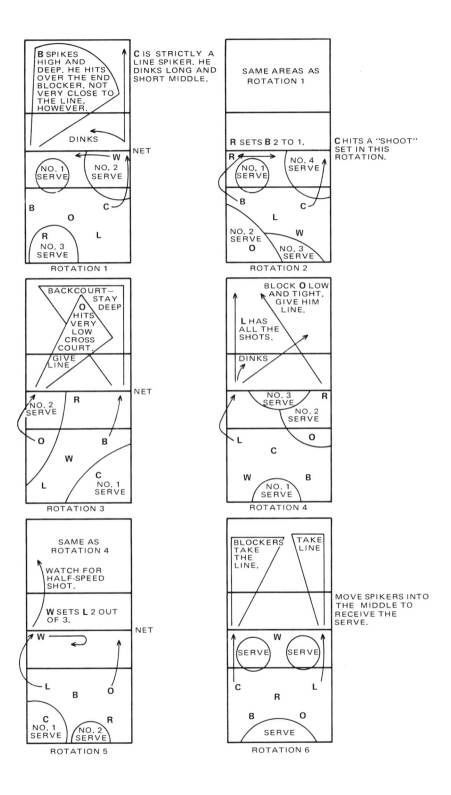

ROTATION 1

B SPIKES HIGH AND DEEP. HE HITS OVER THE END BLOCKER. NOT VERY CLOSE TO THE LINE, HOWEVER.

C IS STRICTLY A LINE SPIKER. HE DINKS LONG AND SHORT MIDDLE.

DINKS

NET

W

NO. 1 SERVE   NO. 2 SERVE

B   C
    O
R   L
NO. 3
SERVE

ROTATION 2

SAME AREAS AS ROTATION 1

R SETS B 2 TO 1.

C HITS A "SHOOT" SET IN THIS ROTATION.

R   NO. 4 SERVE
NO. 1 SERVE

B   C
        L
NO. 2 SERVE   W
        O   NO. 3 SERVE

ROTATION 3

BACKCOURT— STAY DEEP
O HITS VERY LOW CROSS COURT.
GIVE LINE

NET

NO. 2 SERVE   R

O   B
    W
        C
L   NO. 1 SERVE

ROTATION 4

BLOCK O LOW AND TIGHT. GIVE HIM LINE.

L HAS ALL THE SHOTS.

DINKS

NO. 3 SERVE   R
        NO. 2 SERVE

L   O
        C

W   B
    NO. 1 SERVE

ROTATION 5

SAME AS ROTATION 4

WATCH FOR HALF-SPEED SHOT.

W SETS L 2 OUT OF 3.

NET

W

L   O
    B
C   R
NO. 1 SERVE   NO. 2 SERVE

ROTATION 6

BLOCKERS TAKE THE LINE.   TAKE LINE

MOVE SPIKERS INTO THE MIDDLE TO RECEIVE THE SERVE.

W
SERVE   SERVE

C   L
    R
B   O
    SERVE

as possible before he contacts the ball and then move forward. You should get to the 12-ft. line near the side line. Holtzman will be deeper than usual, and you will take some of his normal coverage; B will not hit the ball inside of the 10-ft. line. The set will go to C about one-third of the time. Machado will block the line, even when he's blocking one on one. We may "cheat" Becker toward B and end up with several one-on-one situations here.

Irvin, be alert for the middle dink. The rest of the defenders keep normal spacing, but rotate to your left due to the absence of an effective cross court attack by C.

The defensive scouting report should be handled by the coach subjectively rather than by relying on scouting charts and statistics. Within one match a coach can pick out the ineffective blockers and pick up weaknesses in a team's defense. The defense itself can be easily identified during the match. However, identifying poor diggers and players habitually out of position can be done only if the team being scouted has strong opposition.

The best places to evaluate the blockers are above and behind the referee's stand and behind the blocking team's end line in the center of the court. By watching the match from both vantage points, you can see if the blocker reaches over the net. Lateral arm movement can also be evaluated. The backcourt setter on defense should be watched. Does he leave his position before the ball is spiked to run to the front row and set in the event the ball is dug?

Some players are too slow to cover dink shots and have a tendency to compensate by playing in too close to the net where they cannot possibly dig a ball. Other players squat low to the floor before the ball is hit, or stand flat-footed and do not react fast enough to dive forward to recover a short dink shot.

When scouting the defense, one should observe the following.

- Find the weak blockers
- Identify the types or type of defense used
- Locate the best areas to dink
- Identify the poor diggers

A scoring summary is helpful for the visiting press. If this summary were to be used by the coach, it would have to identify individual players rather than describing events by teams. See Appendix, p. 258.

THE GAME

The team should be taped and in game uniform and sweatsuits at least one hour before game time. Ten minutes should be set aside for reviewing and finalizing the game plan. The coach should be definite and positive in this final recap of game strategy.

If the opposition is strong, the players should know where and to whom they should serve, who are the weak blockers, the opponents' defense and best areas to attack. They should be familiar with the spiking habits and patterns of their opponents and be told what defense they will use. The starting line-up should be announced and any peculiarities of the officials reviewed.

If the match begins at 8:00 P.M., the players should be jogging around the floor by 7:10. The *pre-game warm-up* can be directed by the captain or coach. The players should jog and then go through a team or individual routine of stretching and warm-up exercises for 15 minutes. By 7:25 they should pair up with two players to one ball and set, pass and play pepper until about 7:35. The next 15 minutes should be devoted to spiking, serving and receiving. By 7:50 the team should be spiking against a two-man block and getting in a few serves before the introductions begin.

While the team is warming up, the manager should check out the following.

1. Is the microphone working?
2. Are there towels in the visitors' and home locker rooms and on the benches?
3. Have the locker room doors been secured?
4. Are the referee, umpire, announcer, trainer, scorekeeper and linesmen all present?
5. Does the referee have the game ball?

The coach can watch the warm-up while going over the charting assignments with the staff. Before a game match, both teams warm up together until 10 minutes before introductions are to be made, whereupon each team takes the entire court for five minutes. The referee should gather the captains together about one-half hour before game time for the toss of the coin to decide serve, side and the right to the first or second warm-up period.

While both teams are warming up, there may be a few subtleties exchanged among the opponents in the form of bouncing spikes off opposing setters and displays of spiking prowess designed to impress the opposition. This activity is usually exchanged between the younger members of the team while the veterans concentrate on the percentage shots they intend to use in competition instead of the straight-down warm-up spikes that are usually blocked for a point.

Some teams are so awed at watching their opponents warming up that they lose the match before it begins. It is a simple matter for the setter to place the ball about a foot over the opponents' court to allow a spiker to drive the ball straight down. Some teams attempt to dominate the shared court by using three setters and a left, center and right spiking line giving the opposition no alternative but to spend its time getting hit or dodging spikes.

The *starting rotation* is very important because of the various match-ups and mismatches that may occur. For example, a player may be convinced that he cannot handle an opponent's serve in the left back position and will be useless if the coach matches him up with that server. Some blockers have certain spikers convinced they cannot hit the ball past the block, and other spikers simply cannot be stopped by certain blocking combinations.

More than one crucial match has been lost by a coach leaving his line-up form within plain view for his opponents to observe. A good precaution is to personally hand line-ups to the scorer about 10 minutes before game time. He will check the line-up for form and record it. There should be no confusion regarding the serve since the referee or umpire should hold the toss of the coin well ahead of the time line-ups are to be filled out.

USVBA LINE-UP FORM (per Rule 3.62)

Team_____   Match No._____

Please note: Write only the players' numbers in the positions in which they will *start*. Mark the Captain—C.

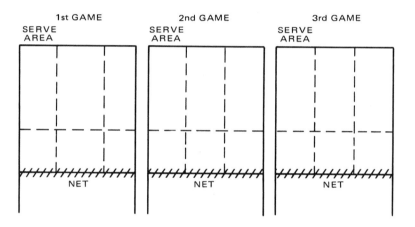

It is good practice to jot down the opposition's starting rotation as the umpire lines up the team prior to the start of the game. In the first game, most coaches fall into the habit of either starting their best spiker in the left front position regardless of which team wins the serve, or arranging their line-up so that their best server serves first. If their team wins the serve, this means the ace server is in the right back position; when the opponent serves first, the best server starts in the right front position and rotates to serve first when the team gets a side out. Other common tactics include placing the best passer in the right back or starting a backcourt specialist in the right back.

A team is allowed twelve substitutions per game, and each player is allowed three entries in every game providing a re-entry in the same position. If a game plan called for dividing one position between a strong spiker in the front court and a strong digger in the backcourt, the player who can make the greatest contribution to the team should start on the bench since the third time the player enters the game, he must stay in unless the coach wishes to put a third player in that position.

If a coach wins the first game, he usually keeps the same starting line-up or moves the rotation back or forward one position, depending on whose turn it is to serve. When the opposing coach loses badly, he usually starts new players or starts the team in different rotations to try new match-ups. When an opponent has been well scouted, it is always good procedure to have all of the opponents' rotations and your intended match-ups written down so that quick decisions regarding new line-ups or substitutions can be made.

After introductions have been made, it is good practice to have the entire team form a *pre-game* huddle in front of the bench for any last minute instructions and to re-emphasize important points. All players need to be included so that everyone is aware of the strategy being used when they enter the game.

Teams should change their strategy during the game to meet the situation. As the opponents' strengths, weaknesses and strategy become evident, it is wise to make changes in your own play to take maximum advantage of the situation. Even the best game plans must be changed to counter strong players and alignments and to exploit weak spots. Strong blockers should be switched to positions where they can combat the strong spikes of the opposing team.

If the coach sees that a spiker is scoring by hitting the ball down the line, the blockers must be signaled to block the line and force the opponent to hit cross court. At the same time, the backcourt defense should be realigned so that the best digger is assigned to the area where the block is channeling the hit. Many times an experienced captain can make changes when the ball is dead and save a charged time out.

Occasionally, a team leader develops with the ability to choose an opportune time to switch defenses during the course of a rally. Most players understand that a change in defense is in order if the opposition is scoring on the present alignment, but very few can choose that precise moment to switch from the middle back to middle in defense when the opposing spiker is tiring or out of position for a set and likely to dink or use a half-speed shot.

When the captain is in the front row, the signal for the switch must be verbal. When the defense learns to play together as a cohesive unit, the backcourt can change alignment by letting the center back player change positions during a rally, with the other backcourt players following his lead. The opposition will not recognize a defensive switch during a rally and will usually direct the ball to an area it has found open earlier in the game—only to have the ball passed by a newly assigned defensive player.

A strong outside blocker who has just blocked his opponent may sense that the spiker will not be set again on the next play. When this situation occurs, the blocker should take the initiative of changing assignments with a weaker teammate in order to align himself with the spiker who is going to receive the set.

Substitutes can be used as messengers to change offensive and defensive tactics if the coach is not willing to use a time out or has no time outs remaining. While on the bench, the substitute should study the players' assignments and match-ups that are in his positions. Serving specialists should study the opponents for passing weaknesses. Blocking and spiking specialists should study the opponents' favorite attack patterns and look for weaknesses in the defense. Defensive backcourt specialists should familiarize themselves with the opposition's spiking habits.

As soon as the coach perceives that a player is starting to lose his effectiveness, he should signal the appropriate substitute or substitutes to warm up on the side line. Substitutes should also share in this responsibility and exercise on the side line whenever they feel themselves getting cold. A common tactic is to direct the action to the player coming off the bench in an attempt to force errors before the substitute can warm up and get in the groove.

Changing the strategy of the game during a 30-second *time out* requires a clear explanation of the most important variables in that particular game. The able coach will soon realize which players, if any, can contribute useful suggestions during time outs; he will learn quickly to evaluate and put into action suggestions that will win games.

Some teams may not develop adequate leadership on the playing floor and must totally rely on signals from the bench to supplement important strategy dispersed during the brief time-out period. When the opponent calls time out to stop your momentum, caution your server to take a little off the first serve to make sure it does not hit the net or go out of bounds. Then the server can come back with a tough serve after the first point.

The rest period between games is 3 minutes. Before the 3 minutes are up, the coach, manager or captain should give the scorer the written form with the starting players in their starting rotations. Line-ups cannot be changed after the referee has given the signal for the teams to take their positions on the court. If a team or coach is confused regarding the line-up, positions may be requested from the scorer when the ball is dead.

During the 3-minute period between games, substitutes may warm up on the court and starting players may leave the court. The coach should quickly check the charts the assistants have kept for him during this period, decide on the starting line-up and gather the team together for instructions regarding the next game.

If conditions allow, the coach should talk briefly to the players being replaced. Many times players do not understand why they are taken out of the line-up. A quick explanation can often straighten out a potential misunderstanding.

A coach can be a great teacher, a good organizer and a thorough conditioner; but, if he fails to select the best players in the proper positions, makes untimely substitutions, does not utilize his time outs and uses the wrong strategy, he will not be a winner. Many of the coaches who fail between the practice session and the game can be classified into several different catagories.

The *indecisive coach* may have a good game plan with a lot of variables that never become clear to the team. After scouting the opposition and finding a player who cannot pass an easy serve, his instructions may be relayed like this, "If you get a chance, serve No. 10." Once the game begins he may ask the person sitting closest to him what he should do next. He continually has substitutes warming up but can never find the strategic moment to put them in the game. He will only substitute if a player injures himself or asks to be taken out of the game.

The *over-enthusiastic coach* reacts to the play like an ardent fan. He moans, cheers and yells at the officials, opposition and his players. During the time outs, he slaps his players on their backs and is terribly exhausted at the end of the match. He never discusses the game until he sees the charts because he is so involved with the last play he cannot remember why his team won or lost.

The *morale crusher* is usually a strict disciplinarian and ardent egotist. Physical mistakes are not allowed on his team; any offender is immediately removed from the game and given a stern lecture. His teams are characterized by a lack of aggressiveness because his players are inclined to avoid the ball so they will not make mistakes.

The *faint heart* cannot bear to watch the action in crucial situations. Overwrought with emotional involvement, he withdraws by shutting his eyes or lapsing into a stupor while the team captain takes the responsibility of making all of the right judgments when the going gets tough. This approach can be successful when the captain is more knowledgeable than the coach.

The *relaxed spectator* is thoroughly aware of what is happening on the court but believes in predestination. He rarely calls a time out or makes a substitution to stop the opponent's momentum because he believes the best team will always win.

The *athlete* is usually a coach who did not quite master the fundamentals of the game in his competitive years but still believes in demonstrating to his players exactly how it is done. He usually closely supervises all aspects of the team warm-up before the contest and personally sets all of his spikers prior to competition. Of course, his setters do not touch the ball for 20 minutes before game time, but the coach gets a change to maintain *his* "touch" on the ball while giving last-minute encouragement to the hitters. Rival coaches have noticed that his setters always seem to make several errors early in the first game of their match.

Mr. Percentage does not seem capable of grasping the psychological aspects of volleyball. Early in the first game he may send in a serving substitute for a spiker who has just put away seven straight spikes and has sparked his team to a fever pitch. The spiker may not serve and pass as well as the substitute, but he is a big part of the team's momentum and should stay in. By the time he returns to the game, he may lose that hot streak and be just another hitter. This coach will also take out the substitute who in three backcourt rotations has made three perfect passes and five diving saves while firing the team and himself up to great heights. This lets the substitute know that regardless of how great a job he does in his speciality, he will never be given a chance to play more than a few rotations in a crucial situation.

Successful volleyball coaches who are capable of making the right decisions in competition seem to be able to exhibit an outward calmness and assurance that draws the confidence of their players. All instructions before the game and during time outs are given in a positive, decisive manner even though the coach may be inwardly unsure of himself. Most important, the successful coach has learned to blend percentage volleyball with the psychology of the moment. He never interrupts or slows down his team's momentum to change strategy, insert substitutes or call time outs. Conversely, he chooses opportune times to slow the momentum of the opposition by substituting players to force the opponent to change successful patterns of attack. Regardless of the situation, he can always take a few seconds to speak to the player being substituted out of the game. This habit of speaking briefly to players coming out of the contest often stops morale problems before they develop.

The successful coach knows the capabilities of his players and recognizes their limitations. He realizes that certain players need to be encouraged whereas others must be calmed down so that rampant emotions do not adversely affect the tactics of the game plan. He realizes that some starting players play better after a brief rest on the bench whereas others lose their touch and rhythm. To sum it up, the winning coach knows the capabilities, idiosyncracies and limitations of his players and helps them to win matches by controlling the tempo of the game and utilizing his players' skills to the team's fullest advantage.

REFERENCE

Daimatsu, Hirobumi *Follow Me*. The author was the 1964 Japanese Women's Olympic Coach.

BIBLIOGRAPHY

Cohen, Harlan. *Power volleyball drills*. 1967. Creative Sports Book, P. O. Box 2244, Hollywood, Calif. 90028. $2.00
Diagrammed handbook of drills.

Pictorial volleyball. 1966. Creative Sport Books, P. O. Box 2244, Hollywood, Calif., 90028.
A series of 26 photos, 8 1/2 by 11, showing volleyball skills and positioning. Printed descriptions of mechanics. Presents clear sequential shots of a woman performing the underhand serve, overhand serve, chest pass, dig pass, set-up, spike and dink. Also illustrations of team play. Loose leaf for posting.

Shondell, Donald S. (Ed.) *Official Rules and Reference Guide*. United States Volleyball Association, P. O. Box 109, Berne, Ind. 46711.
Presents a complete summary of past season, rules for coming season. Many informational and interesting articles.

Wilson, Harry E. (Ed.) International volleyball review. P. O. Box 554, Encino, Calif. 91316. $2.00/year
Published for more than 25 years. Reports all local, regional and national tourna-

ments and publishes articles from throughout the world, including feature stories and articles on trends and events.

FILM

Volleyball. Official volleyball films of NCAA-AAHPER. Produced by Ealing/ Sports Illustrated. Cartridged Super 8 mm. motion pictures. Set, $149.70. Individual loops of the serve, forearm pass, overhand set, spike, block, and dive and roll can be purchased for $24.95. Ealing Film Loops, 2225 Massachusetts Ave., Cambridge, Mass. 02140.

These are instructional films, authored by Allen E. Scates. Young All American and Olympic players demonstrate technically flawless volleyball fundamentals in slow motion analysis and freeze frame at critical teaching points. Demonstrates and describes the basic skills necessary to play competitive or recreational volleyball.

DIAGRAM OF VOLLEYBALL COURT

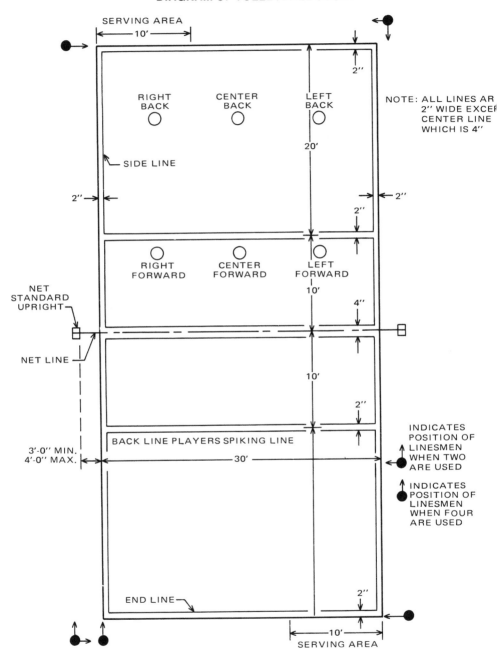

Reprinted with permission of the editor. Donald S. Shondell (Ed.). 1971 *Official volleyball guide*. Berne, Ind.: United States Volleyball Association.

APPENDIX

OFFICIAL HAND SIGNALS

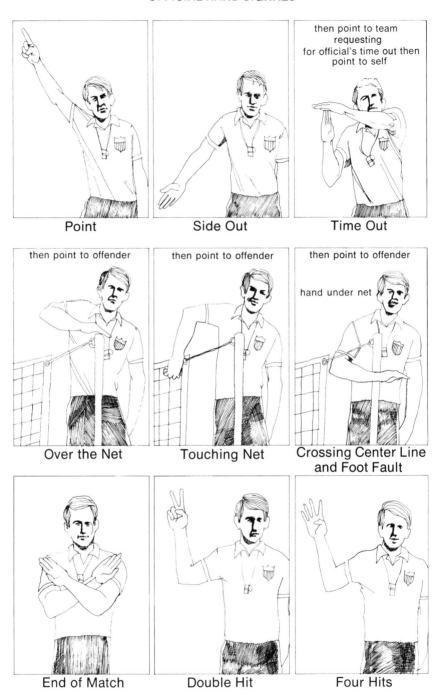

Point   Side Out   Time Out

then point to team requesting
for official's time out then
point to self

then point to offender   then point to offender   then point to offender

hand under net

Over the Net   Touching Net   Crossing Center Line
and Foot Fault

End of Match   Double Hit   Four Hits

Used with permission. Donald S. Shondell (Ed.). 1971 *Official volleyball guide.*
Berne, Ind.: United States Volleyball Association.

sweeping motions of arm and hand twice

close fingers twice

Thrown Ball

Held Ball

Lifted Ball

Out of Position

Technical Foul

point thumbs up

Double Foul

rotate hands

Substitution

ball in

ball out

Linesman's Signals

COLLEGE VOLLEYBALL QUESTIONNAIRE

If space is insufficient for full answers, please use the reverse side of page.

Name _____ Nickname _____

    First   Middle   Last

Campus Address _____ Campus Phone _____

Home Address _____ Home Phone _____

Height _____ Weight _____ Age _____ Date of Birth _____

Military Status and Draft Classification _____

Married _____ Wife's Name _____ Children Age(s) ____

Shoe Size _____ Waist Size _____ Jersey Size _____

Month and Year Entered This School _____

College _____ Major _____ Class _____

                                                             F, S, J, Sr.

Fraternity or Clubs _____

Business or Professional Objectives _____

Years of eligibility remaining, including present season __

When will you graduate? Quarter _____ Year _____

List volleyball experience in high school, clubs, open teams, Armed Services _____

_____

How many seasons of college volleyball have you played? ____

Colleges, universities and/or junior colleges attended. List names, dates and athletic achievements _____

_____

Prominent relatives in athletics _____

Your biggest thrill in sports _____

_____

Who is the greatest volleyball player you ever played against? _____

_____

Who is the greatest volleyball player you ever saw? _____

Why did you choose this college? _____

_____

SCHEDULING TOURNAMENTS AND MATCHES

The traditional method of conducting local volleyball competition in the United States is to hold a double elimination tournament with a winners' bracket for undefeated teams and a losers' bracket for teams that have lost one match. Teams that lose two matches are eliminated from the tournament. The finals pit the winner of the winners' bracket against the winner of the losers' bracket. When the team in the losers' bracker defeats its opponent in the final match, a one-game double finals is scheduled to determine the champion, since both teams have lost one match. In a double finals playoff the final match consists of one game. The USVBA uses the double elimination method and conducts its national championships in the mens, womens, senior and collegiate divisions.

Recently, major regional tournaments have borrowed some aspects of major international or world tournaments and schedule single round robin tournaments in "pools" or separate brackets. For example, if twenty teams were competing in a tournament, they would be divided into four pools of five teams apiece. The top four teams would be placed in separate pools as well as teams five through eight. The rest of the teams would depend on the luck of the draw for their placement. If the tournament was scheduled for one day, the teams would play a two-game round robin schedule; the top two finishers would compete in a single elimination finals and the rest of the pool would be eliminated. Winners and runners-ups would then be seeded into an eight-team single elimination bracket for the championships.

It is possible to have over 60 teams competing at the same site in one day. When there are large numbers of participants, it is suggested that a rating committee be formed to rate players into A and AA categories. There should be periodic meetings of the committee to re-evaluate performance and make changes in individual ratings. Any player should be free to appeal his rating to an executive committee if he disagrees with the rating committee's judgment. AA players should be prohibited from playing in all A competitions. An alternate method is to still have two divisions of play but to rate entire teams instead of individual players.

As volleyball increases in popularity, and as competitions become more frequent and crowded (with players and spectators), the present tournament setup is becoming outmoded and very impractical.

Tournaments usually start at 9:00 A.M. and finish as late as 1:00 A.M. the next morning. In other countries teams never play more than one five-game match against a single opponent on the same day. One day tournaments in the United States develop poor playing habits among players because players tend to "pace" themselves so that they will have enough energy to play in the finals. Space is usually at such a premium that play is often held up while players or balls from other courts come careening into the playing area.

Referees become fatigued and lose their sharpness and ability to control the game. Publicity is virtually nonexistent because the morning paper's deadline has passed before the tournament is completed and newspapers are not interested in printing a story that is a day late.

Most of the players, officials and fans in the United States are in favor of changing the structure of volleyball competition from tournaments to *leagues*. Since 1963 the Southern California Intercollegiate Volleyball Association (SCIVA) has been conducting *league matches* between schools in the same area which have relative playing ability. Publicity and attendance at SCIVA matches have improved tremendously over the years. Fans have identified with a college team, and crowds of 4,000 to 5,000 are not uncommon at some of the larger campuses. Local papers publish stories before and after the match and SCIVA standings are publicized.

This collegiate league has drawn excellent athletes, a great number of spectators and additional money to support the program. Consequently, SCIVA teams have become stronger, coaches are better organized and SCIVA players have been selected to national teams. Recently, radio and television have covered the more important matches.

The organization of SCIVA is quite simple. Varsity matches are played at 8:00 P.M. and consist of three out of five games with no time limit. The larger schools conduct junior varsity matches which begin at 6:30 P.M. and consist of two out of three games with no time limit. Players go all out and the fans leave at the end of the match anticipating the next league contest.

The coaches from the member schools meet once a year to select the commissioner of the league, who draws up the yearly schedule and handles all conflicts which may occur. Eligibility rules do not present a problem since all athletic departments file with the commissioner, a certificate of eligibility of their team members according to NCAA rules and regulations. The commissioner then forwards a copy of each competing school's eligibility report to member coaches. If an eligibility question arises, the commissioner contacts the athletic director at the involved school.

A head referee is selected to assign officials to all league matches. Each member school pays one fee ($15) to the head referee at the beginning of the season and another to the assigned officials during home matches. The referee receives $15 per match; the umpire, $10; scorer, $5; and both linesmen, $5. The cost amounts to $40 per match.

Roster forms are exchanged before the matches. Coaches sign the score sheet and rate the officials and outstanding players. Then, the sheet is forwarded to the commissioner.

As soon as several strong teams are developed in a given district, it becomes necessary to hold a district tournament to qualify teams for the national tournament. The initial selection of teams for the district tournament is made by a district advisory committee which submits its recommendations to the National Volleyball Tournament Committee. The advisory committee uses the following criteria to select teams for the district tournament:

- Won-lost record
- Strength of schedule

● Eligibility of athletes for the National Volleyball Championships

Each team selected to compete in the district tournament files certification of its team members' eligibility in accordance with the sponsoring organization's rules and regulations. Qualifying teams are seeded by the advisory committee on the basis of playing record and strength of schedule. Final approval of the seedings should be made by a national volleyball tournament committee. If eight teams are selected it is suggested that they be placed in one of two four-team pools on the basis of positions assigned in the seeding process:

Pool A   Seeds 1, 3, 5 and 7

Pool B   Seeds 2, 4, 6 and 8

Each four-team pool plays a round robin match schedule. A match consists of two games out of three to 15 points, or 8 minutes of ball-in play time—whichever occurs first. However, a team must gain a 2-point advantage to win. The first two teams in each pool will qualify for a seeded four-team single elimination playoff. The game ball should be the same one that is used in the national championships.

If there are less than six outstanding teams in a given district, other types of playoffs should be used. In a five-team district playoff, a two- out of three-game single round robin tournament is best. Each team can play two matches the first day and two more the second day. If two teams tie for a qualification spot on the basis of matches won and lost, the following methods can be used to break the tie.

1. The team that defeated the other in round robin play will receive the top selection or qualifying spot.

2. If more than two teams are tied, the difference between the total number of games won and total number of games lost will be obtained. The team with the greater differential will be selected.

Example:

Team	Match Record	Game Record	Differential
A	2–2	4–4	0
B	2–2	5–6	−1
C	2–2	6–5	+1

Conclusion: Team C was selected because of the won-lost differential of one game.

3. If two or more teams remain tied after applying the above criteria, the difference between the total number of points scored and points given up will be obtained. The team with the greater differential will be selected.

When teams travel great distances to play one another, a special type of tournament can be arranged to insure adequate participation by the weakest team. In other words, if a weak team has traveled a few thousand miles to compete against stronger teams, the tournament host should not schedule a single or double elimination tournament and send the visitor home after one or two matches. Meaningful competition can be scheduled the first day by conducting a single round robin tournament for the purposes of seeding for the second day's competition. The second day's schedule might look like this:

11:00 A.M.	First seed vs. fourth seed (best 3 out of 5)
12:30 P.M.	Second seed vs. third seed (best 3 out of 5)
7:00 A.M.	Third place match (best 2 out of 3)
8:00 P.M.	Championship match (best 3 out of 5)

The advantage of this type of competition is that the poorer team may lose every game and still play in eleven games. The stronger teams may play hard the first day in the hopes of being seeded number 1 so that they can play the weakest team in the final day's competition.[1]

The following is a scoring summary (see three tables) of an NCAA volleyball championship match held at UCLA's Pauley Pavilion on April 25, 1970. The match was attended by over 3,000 fans.

CSLB	UCLA	Notes	CSLB	UCLA	Notes
	1	spiked into net		1	spiked out by CSLB
1		spiked out		2	Holtzman dink
2					
			1		Holtzman spike out
	2	service ace	2		UCLA mishandled ball
	3	ball dug and put away	3		UCLA mishandled ball
3				3	Machado dig, Irvin spike
	4	blocked spike		4	Kilgour spike
	5	ball hit out		5	Kilgour block
	6	Becker spike		6	ball out by LB
	7	Becker-Holtzman block		7	ball out by LB
	8	Kilgour spike after long rally		8	ball out by LB
	9	Kilgour spikes hard		9	Becker hits ball off blockers
	10	Irvin spike		10	ball out by LB
	11	Holtzman spike		11	ball out by LB
4		Johnson good serve	4		double contact by UCLA
5		UCLA spikes out		12	ball out by LB
6		Imwalle block		13	ball out after great rally
7		Chowen dink		14	CSLB called for throwing
	12	CSLB called for carrying ball		15	spiked out
	13	spiker netted			
	14	ball out			
	15	net violation on CSLB; UCLA Wins First			

UCLA wins, 15-7   UCLA wins, 15-4

CSLB	UCLA	Notes
	1	Kilgour spike
	2	Machado dig, Kilgour spike
1		UCLA overlapping in rotation
2		net by Becker
	3	held ball called on LB
3		ball out
	4	double contact called on LB
	5	net violation by LB
4		ball hit outside tape
	6	block by Herring-Kilgour
	7	block by Machado
	8	Machado spike
	9	Becker dink
	10	ball out
5		Parker spike
	11	ball out
	12	Holtzman dig, Irvin spike
	13	ball hit off blocker by Irvin
6		ball out by UCLA
	14	Irvin-Zajec block
7		ball out by UCLA
8		net by UCLA
	15	Holtzman dink

UCLA wins, 15-8

Thus, UCLA won the first NCAA volleyball championship match. For more information concerning the tables on pp. 258 and 259, the reader is advised to refer to Harold T. Friermood's "Cumulative record of volleyball championship winners" which appears in the *1969 Official Volleyball Guide* (Berne, Ind.: USVBA). See pages 105–121.

FIVB Men's World Volleyball Championship Winners

Number	Year	Place	Number of Teams	Winner	Runner-Up	(USA)
1	1949	Prague	10	USSR	Czechoslovakia	-
2	1952	Moscow	11	USSR	Czechoslovakia	-
3	1956	Paris	24	Czechoslovakia	Romania	(6th)
4	1960	Sao Paulo, Brazil	12	USSR	Czechoslovakia	(6th)
5	1962	Moscow	10	USSR	Czechoslovakia	-
6	1966	Prague	22	Czechoslovakia	Romania	(11th)
7	1970	Sofia	23	East Germany	Bulgaria	(18th)

FIVB Women's World Volleyball Championship Winners

Number	Year	Place	Number of Teams	Winner	Runner-Up	(USA)
1	1952	Moscow	8	USSR	Poland	-
2	1956	Paris	17	USSR	Romania	(9th)
3	1960	Sao Paulo, Brazil	10	USSR	Japan	(6th)
4	1962	Moscow	8	Japan	USSR	-
5	1967	Tokyo	4	Japan	USA	(2nd)
6	1970	Varna	22	USSR	Japan	(11th)

Pan American Games Men's Volleyball Championship Winners*

Number	Year	Place	Winner	Runner-Up
1	1955	Mexico City	USA	Mexico
2	1959	Chicago	USA	Brazil
3	1963	Sao Paulo, Brazil	Brazil	USA
4	1967	Winnipeg, Man. Can.	USA	Brazil
5	1971	Cali, Columbia	Cuba	USA
6	1975	Santiago, Chile		

* Volleyball not included in the first Pan Am Games (1951).

Pan American Games Women's Volleyball Championship Winners*

Number	Year	Place	Winner	Runner-Up
1	1955	Mexico City	Mexico	USA
2	1959	Chicago	Brazil	USA
3	1963	Sao Paulo, Brazil	Brazil	USA
4	1967	Winnipeg, Man. Can.	USA	Peru
5	1971	Cali, Columbia	Cuba	Peru
6	1975	Santiago, Chile		

* Volleyball not included in the first Pan Am Games (1951).

Olympic Games Men's Volleyball Championship Winners*

Number	Year	Place	Number of Teams	Winner	Runner-Up	(USA)
1	1964	Tokyo	10	USSR	Czechoslovakia	9th
2	1968	Mexico City	10	USSR	Japan	7th
3	1972	Munich	12			
4	1976	Montreal				

* Volleyball not included in Olympic Games (1896–1960).

Olympic Games Women's Volleyball Championship Winners*

Number	Year	Place	Number of Teams	Winner	Runner-Up	(USA)
1	1964	Tokyo	6	Japan	USSR	6th
2	1968	Mexico City	8	USSR	Japan	8th
3	1972	Munich	10			
4	1976	Montreal				

* Volleyball not included in Olympic Games (1896–1960).

REFERENCE

[1]For a detailed analysis of tournament seedings and procedures, see Boyden, Douglas, and Burton, Roger. 1957. *Staging successful tournaments.* New York: Association Press. Also, for information about running a tournament or clinic, photos for publicity purposes, sample news releases and volleyball records, write to G. R. McDonald, National Public Information Director, National Volleyball Information Center, 5142 Tujunga, No. Hollywood, Calif. 91601.

Index

Analyzing Attack by Spiking Position
  chart, 239
Arm strength in dive, 157
Amateur Athletic Union (AAU), 4, 14
Attack (*see also* Offense):
  center, stopping, 198-200
  five-one, 182
  six-two (*see* Attack, three-hitter)
  three-hitter, 170-182, 192-193
  two-hitter, 163, 189
Attack Chart, 237

Back:
  left:
    in middle back defense, 186
    in middle in defense, 196-197
  middle, 186
  right:
    in middle back defense, 186
    in middle in defense, 193, 196
Ball:
  in beach doubles, 208
  "dead", 209
  free, 192, 201
  moving to, 40-43
    in dig, 154-155
  official, 208
  valve placement in serve, 23-25
Beach doubles (*see* Doubles, beach)
Block, 105-134
  attack, 115-116
  body position for, 108, 112
  definition of, 105
  down, 191
  false weakness in, 127-128
  one-step approach to, 112
  seeing, 77, 81
  soft, 116-119
  standing takeoff in, 108, 112
  three-man, 121
  two-man, 105, 119-124
Block rebounds, 169, 221
Blocker:
  end, 120-121
    in middle back defense, 184-185
    in middle in defense, 193
  middle, 121-124, 126-127, 197-198
  off-:
    in middle back defense, 185-186
    in middle in defense, 197
Blocking:
  common errors, 130-131
  endurance, 220

game situation drills, 133-134
  individual technique, 105-114
  strategy, 124-128
  teaching progression, 131-133
  three-man, 188-189
  two-man, 188
  vertical jump in, 108-114
Brown, Elwood S., 4

Captain, 245
Catholic Youth Organization (CYO), and
  volleyball, 15
Charts, 233-239
Coach:
  philosophy of, 229-230
  responsibilities of, 229-248
  types of, 229-230, 246-248
Coeducational play, 203-206
  defense in, 205-206
  offense in, 203-205
  rules for, 203
Conditioning, 215-227
  programs for, 215-221
  technique, 220-221
Crossover step in blocking, 121-124

Defense, 182-202
  backcourt, 220
  changing, 201-202
  in coeducational play, 205-206
  in doubles, 207
  middle back, 183-186
    to offense, 189-193
  middle in, 193-198
    to offense, 201
  starting positions in, 183
  technique of, individual, 135-158
Dig, 45
  backhand, 147, 157-158
  body position, 153
  definition of, 32
  high, 137
  left-hand, 153
  one-arm, 141
  overhand, 146-147, 209-210
  rolling, 3, 136, 141, 155
  running, 220
  and set, 64, 67
Dink, 85-89
  definition of, 85
  with knuckles, 89
  over middle blocker, 85
  open-hand, 12, 89, 209

two-handed, 89
Dive, 3, 147-153, 220
  front, 151-153
  learning, 157-158
Division for Girls' and Women's Sports
  (DGWS), 14
Doubles, 206-207
  beach, 207-210
  rules for, 208-210
  defense in, 207
  offense in, 206-207
  rules for, 206
Drills:
  blocking, 133-134
  pepper, 158
  serving, 29-30
  spiking, 97-103

End blocker, 120-121
Errors, 233-238
Exercises:
  endurance, 218
  general, 215-218
  strength, 217-218
  stretching, 216-217

Federation of International Volleyball (see
  International Volleyball Federation)
Free ball, 192, 201

Game, 242-248
  plan for, 242-243
  pre-game huddle, 245
  pre-game warm-up, 243
  starting rotation, 243-244
  strategy changes during, 245

Halstead, Alfred T., 4
Hand signals, official, 252-253
High schools, volleyball in, 4, 15
Home Team Receiving Chart, 235
Huddle, pre-game, 245

Individual Error Chart, 235
International competition, 15-16
International Volleyball Federation
  (FIVB), 5, 15-16

Jumping ability, increasing, 218-220

Leagues, 256
  collegiate
Left back:
  in middle back defense, 186
  in middle in defense, 196-197

M-Formation, 162-170
  in co-educational play, 203
Middle back, 186
Middle blocker, 121-124, 126-127
Middle in, 196
  set by, 68
Mintonette (see Volleyball)
Morgan, William G., 4, 5-6
Mormons, and volleyball, 15

National Association of Intercollegiate
  Athletics (NAIA), 4, 14
National Collegiate Athletic Association
  (NCAA), 4, 13-14

Odeneal, William T., 5

Offense, 163-182 (see also Attack)
  alignment in, four-two, 163)
  in coeducational play, 203-205
  in doubles play, 206-207
Olympic games, volleyball in, 3, 5, 15
Opponent Passing Chart, 237
Overweight, 217-218

Pass, 31-46, 170
  arm position, 34-37
  elbow lock, 34, 37, 137
  elbow snap, 37
  backward, 46
  body position in, 40
  unexpected, 46
  "bump", 34
  changing direction in, 43
  definition of, 31
  forearm, 32, 136
  hand position for, 32-34
  clenched-fist, 33
  curled-fingers, 34
  thumb-over-palm, 34
  lateral, 43
  one-arm, 45 (see also Dig)
  overhand, 31, 136
  from unexpected positions, 46
Passing:
  backing up in, 167-169
  techniques in, 38-40
Pepper drill, 158
Philosophy, coach's, 229-230
Pivot and drive in blocking, 123-124
Play sets:
  one-set, 174-175
  four-set, 176
  three-set, 176
  two-set, 175-176
Players:
  qualifications of, 178-179
  training and conditioning of, 215-227
  warm-up, 243
Practice, 225-227, 230-232
  orientation, 231-232
  schedules for, 225-226
Pre-game huddle, 245
Pre-game warm-up, 243

Referee:
  in beach doubles, 208
  in league matches, 256
Rest period between games, 246
Right back:
  in middle back defense, 186
  in middle in defense, 193, 196
Roll and dig, 136, 141, 155
Rules:
  changes in, 6-9
  effects of, 9-11
  eligibility, understanding, 232
  history of, 5-9
  interpretations of, effects of, 11-12

Sargent Jump Test, 108-109
Scoring summary, 242
Scouting report:
  defensive, 242
  offensive, 240
Scouting and statistics, 233-242
Screw under step, 40, 43
Serve, 21-30
  overhand:

floater, 23-25
  spin, 25-26, 210
overhand pass of, 11
round house:
  floater, 26-28
  spin, 28
sky ball, 210
underhand, 22-23
Serve-receiving chart (see Home Team
  Receiving Chart)
Serve reception, 173
  patterns and plays in, 179-182
  cross, 180
  four-man, 179-180
  tandem, 180-181
  thirty-one, 180-181
Service area, 22, 32
Serving, drills in, 29-30
Set, 49-68
  back, 53
  long, 64
  move forward and, 66
  short, 64, 65
  backcourt, 64, 67
  crosscourt:
    four players, 63
    three players, 63
  decision, 65
  definition of, 49
  and dig, 64, 67
  forearm, 49
  four-, 176
  front, 51, 66
  jump, 57, 65, 176, 220
  lateral, 53-55, 66-67
  by middle in, 68
  normal, 50
  one-, 174-175
  with one ball to two players, 62
  overhand, 49-50
  on run, 63
  or spike, 66
  three-, 176
  traditional position for, 55-57
  two-, 175-176
Setter:
  back row, 171-173
  blocking left, 189-190
  blocking right, 190
  qualifications of, 178
Setting:
  facing stronger hitter in, 167
  for specialists, 65-68
  strategy in, 57-60
  switching in, 166-167
  teaching progression, 60-68
Shoot (see Play sets, four-set)
"Short court" rule, 206
Slide step, 40, 43
  in blocking, 120, 121-122
  in digging, 155
Southern California Intercollegiate Volleyball Association (SCIVA), 256
Spaulding Volleyball Rule Book, 4
Specialists, 224, 245-246
Spike, 69-103
  approach for, 71-75
  hop takeoff, 72, 74
  one-leg takeoff, 74-75
  step-close takeoff, 72, 74
  in coeducational play, 203
  definition of, 69

endurance, 220
force of, 77
half-speed, 12
with heel of hand, 77
of low vertical set, 90-94
off-hand, 71, 119
  of back one-set, 94
off-speed, 89
of one-set, 90-94
on-hand, 71, 119, 171
with palm, 77
passing of overhand, 209-210
reading of, 128-130
round house, 84-85
of shoot set, 96
soft (see Dink)
topspin of, 77
trajectory of, 75, 77
of two-set, 93
vertical wipe-off, 84
Spiker, qualifications of, 179
Spiking:
  backcourt, 221
  backing up in, 169-170, 176-178
  center, defensing, 186-189
  drills in, 97-103
Spiking efficiency formula, 237-238
Spiking Efficiency by Game Chart, 239
Squat, 40
  angle of, in block, 108, 112
  in digging, 154
Stance, digger's, 136-137
Statistics and scouting, 233-242
Substitutes, 224-225, 245-246

Team Error Charts, 233
Team standards, understanding, 232
Technique player, 172-173
  qualifications of, 178
Theories:
  of endurance training, 219
  of overload, 219
  of specificity, 219
  of strength training, 219
Times out, 246
Tournaments:
  district, 256-258
  double elimination, 255
  local, 255
  and matches scheduling, 255-261
  one-day, 255-256
  regional, major, 255
Training:
  and conditioning, 215-227
  schedules for:
    daily, 226
    weekly, 225-226
Training cycle, seasonal, 221-225
  competitive phase of, 224-225
  conditioning phase of, 221-222
  preparatory phase of, 223-224
  practice outlines for, 226-227
  special phases of, 225

United States Collegiate Sports Council
  (USCSC), 16
United States Olympic Committee, 15
United States Volleyball Association
  (USVBA), 4-5, 13

Warm-up, pre-game, 243
Weight-training, 218-220
World University Games, 16